HACKED AGAIN

To Oscar —

Stay Safe

HACKED AGAIN

SCOTT N. SCHOBER

ScottSchober.com Publishing

ISBN-13: 978-0-9969022-0-5
LCCN: 2015921105

Distributed by Itasca Books

Cover Design by Alexander von Ness of Nessgraphica
Illustrations by Jake Thomas of Jake Thomas Creative

Printed in the United States of America

CONTENTS

Part 4: Noteworthy Hacks and Breaches

FOREWORD

by Jon Leiberman

I FIRST MET SCOTT WHEN I INTERVIEWED HIM on my Sirius XM radio show, *Leiberman Live*. We talked about various security concerns and tools that addressed serious issues. We also discussed his new technology that could help teachers catch cheating students in the classroom. I was struck by his honest, easygoing manner and his ability to bring complicated concepts into easy-to-digest ideas. The audience found him compelling and—better yet—down to earth.

I was fascinated to hear of his personal story of being hacked by members of the black hat world who targeted him for revealing ways the Average Joe was being victimized.

Over the next few years, our paths continued to cross. My work as an investigative reporter often overlapped with Scott's. The criminal world was quickly embracing the countless ways that personal data was being shamelessly shared, bought, and sold. Scott was my go-to guy for simplifying the tech jargon for my audience. He *got it,* and he helped them get it, too.

Scott's book holds many first-hand accounts of stories with endings that can be hard to believe. He offers a clear foundation, yet provides a step-by-step guide through this often technically intimidating world. I read the book from cover to cover in one sitting, and immediately changed all my passwords to ones that were stronger. I suggest you do the same. And, I found out that's just the start of what we all need to do to safeguard our personal information.

Scott is a highly authentic source, an innovative business owner, and a sought-after speaker and security expert, and I hold his opinions in high regard. You will enjoy this easy-to-digest yet vitally important book.

Jon

Jon Leiberman's voice has been heard in countless house-holds and vehicles across America. Literally millions of Americans recognize his voice for his work on the Howard Stern Show, America's Most Wanted, *CNN, FOX, and more.*

INTRODUCTION

WITH MY MONDAY-MORNING COFFEE IN HAND, I turned on my computer and began comparing my mental checklist to my digital one for all the items I wanted to accomplish that week. It was late in 2013, and this weekly ritual allowed me to feel a sense of accomplishment as I crossed off each item I completed throughout the day to help me stay focused in my little world of organized chaos.

I am the president and CEO of a privately held wireless engineering corporation that has been in business for more than forty years. Our area of expertise is in wireless and security testing tools. In the last five years, there has been rapid growth in wireless threat-detection tools used by cybersecurity groups globally. In a typical day at the office, I check our online accounts to see where we stand—especially to see if we received any incoming wire transfers, as about twenty-five percent of our business is international.

As I reflect back on that scary day now, I remember entering in my frustratingly long and easy-to-forget password on the banking website only to find the account balance was alarmingly low. My mind raced in disbelief. Did payroll come out? *No, wait, it's only Monday, and payroll is not debited until Thursday.* I found myself looking at numerous debits not at all familiar to me. *What's going on here?* Then reality hit me.

"Hacked . . . again!" I finally had to admit it to myself out loud.

We are a security company and this happened to us? But this was not an isolated incident or even the first time my company had been hacked. For that, we must look back even further to a slightly younger and greener small business and its owner. Between and after our hacks, I have come to learn so much more than I ever would've imagined. I try not to let my mistakes define me so much as guide me and keep me humble. And that brings me to this book and to the idea behind writing it. Hopefully, I will connect with readers eager to learn from my mistakes and my experience in the cybersecurity industry.

I am excited to share my journey with you in the hope it will prevent you from going down same path I have already traversed. In Part 1, I share my candid story of how my small business was the victim of repeated cyberattacks and how I quickly learned that nothing is truly secure. In Part 2, I share best practices to help you protect your identity, business, personal data, and finances by using specific measures, both preventative and remedial. Part 3 is designed to help you stay safe in this challenging and always changing digital world without losing hope or sight of what's truly important. In Part 4, I tally the major breaches that have made the headlines over the past several years and how they affect us all.

I can hardly contain my excitement for the world of technology that I live and work in everyday. I have carved a path for myself as a business owner, inventor, and now a cybersecurity expert, but I have much further to go, and this book serves as a next step in my quest to educate, inform, and, most importantly, help others survive and thrive in this digitally connected world.

PART 1

LEARNING THE HARD WAY

CHAPTER 1

CASH IN THE MATTRESS

FOR SMALL BUSINESSES TO BE COMPETITIVE, they need to align with a strong bank. This allows a company to borrow capital, pay bills, and maintain a trusted source to safely hold valuable funds as their business grows. My parents, Gary and Eileen Schober, opened Berkeley Varitronics Systems's (BVS) bank account back in 1973 at United Jersey Bank in Edison, New Jersey, when I was only four years old.

BVS was one of the very first corporate accounts opened at United Jersey Bank. Back then, it was not uncommon to walk into a bank where everyone knew everyone else and were on a first-name basis. This provided a level of comfort in knowing who was watching your money. There was an implied level of trust when you saw those familiar faces, and you felt secure.

BVS continued to grow, and United Jersey Bank grew as well. United Jersey eventually bought out its rival, Summit Bank out of Summit, New Jersey, but kept the Summit name. In the early 2000s, Summit Bank was acquired by Fleet Boston and kept the name Fleet Bank in New Jersey. By 2005, Fleet Bank was acquired by Bank of America (BoA) in a large transaction. Needless to say, the friendly local bank that BVS trusted for decades has changed significantly: it's now a goliath of a bank, not at all reminiscent of the early days of personalized small business banking.

In 2012, BVS continued to expand its wireless security offerings to security professionals, and I began getting numerous requests for advice about the tools I would recommend to counter wireless threats, as well as general questions on how to keep small businesses safe. As soon as our solutions and advice began to get out into the mainstream, we also found ourselves a target for hackers. Sharing and helping has always been fundamental in my upbringing. Hackers might appreciate advice and scripts from fellow hackers, but I can assure you that they do not appreciate anyone who makes their hacking more difficult by providing advice on protecting businesses from hacks. I was about to find this out the hard way.

It was late in 2012 when I logged onto BVS's Bank of America (BoA) account and noticed multiple unfamiliar transactions. Since we had several debit cards corporate officers used for travel and trade-show expenses, I figured the charges were legitimate, albeit unknown to me. Upon closer inspection, though, I found many charges originated in states where no trade shows were scheduled. Something was not adding up. My eyes began to scan down the screen, seeing transaction after transaction of numerous unfamiliar debits from our account. Disbelief was followed quickly by disgust, and I blurted out the only thing I could see in front of me and the last thing I wanted to hear:

"We've been hacked."

I immediately called our local BoA Edison branch that we have dealt with for decades and reported the breach. They did not seem as upset as I was and told me there was nothing the branch could do. They suggested I call their fraud department to report the breach. I quickly dialed BoA fraud department and was asked numerous questions to validate my credentials before I was assured they would take care of the breach and get our money back. My mind raced, wondering what could have happened. Even though under $10,000 was stolen, it was still a painful ordeal I never wanted to endure again. The process involved writing several letters to the bank and credit-card issuer, along with providing copies of invoices for our legitimate transactions so the fraudulent ones would stick out like a sore thumb.

Trying to prove a transaction is unauthorized is futile, as no documentation ever exists to show what you did *not* do. This process, although lengthy and distracting, provided a valuable lesson to me as a small business owner: It is essential to maintain copies of all banking and customer invoices so that if you ever do suffer a breach, you can quickly work toward resolving it with well-organized documents to back your case. In the end, we jumped through all of the bank's hoops, and after three long months, we received one hundred percent of the stolen funds back.

During those three months, we could not use our company debit cards and waited until they issued new cards. For credit card transactions during that down time, I used my personal card for purchases and was reimbursed from BVS. This proved to be a bad idea, as my personal credit card also became compromised. I realized I was not just the typical consumer being targeted, but that the hackers were now targeting both my company and me as a cybersecurity expert. *This was personal.*

Before I go further, I want to quickly clarify some terms: Almost all credit card users have experienced what the banks and card issuers call fraud, which is why they have fraud departments. But what you may not realize is that all of these fraud claims and thefts are the result of hacks perpetrated by hackers. These might not be the images of hackers we have come to know through popular movies and TV of the evil criminals sitting in front of terminals all day writing code in some dank basement. Hackers don't actually even need a computer, just some basic social skills and the audacity to use someone else's money or identity to steal for themselves. *Social engineering* is an effective tactic hackers employ that involves tricking individuals to break normal security procedures. When someone uses your credit card to make an unauthorized purchase at a retail store or a website, they are socially engineering the situation to fool the store into believing they are you. Some might see it more as a con game or simple theft, but make no mistake: these thieves are manipulating people and policies in order to control the technology behind it all. That is the essence of hacking.

During the investigation of the BVS hack, we discovered our debit card was compromised (meaning a hacker stole our debit card information as we purchased items online) on a website we did not normally frequent. Unauthorized debits appeared all over our bank statement. The hacker took our credit card credentials and sold them on the dark web, along with thousands of other victims' compromised credentials. The dark web is the term for a portion of World Wide Web content that is not indexed by standard search engines and is generally attributed to hacking and illegal cyber-activities. Cyberhackers can search forums in the dark web for particular individuals they want to target, and it seemed likely my name was on their list.

I relentlessly pushed the bank's fraud department to explain what we could have done differently to prevent the breach. They emphasized that we should only deal with companies we know and have worked with in the past. The irony of this statement from BoA was not lost on me. Here we are dealing with a bank that we used to know intimately, and through numerous name changes, buyouts, and mergers became a veritable stranger to BVS for all intents and purposes. Now they are telling me to only deal with people and companies I know and trust. I can understand why many people have lost their faith in banks altogether and store their hard-earned cash under their mattresses. Realizing the pain of moving all our company assets to a different bank, we reluctantly agreed to the bank's recommendations and trudged through the process of getting new cards issued and new passwords. It was back to business as usual—or so I thought.

CHAPTER 2

OPTING INTO CREDIT CARD FRAUD

ACCEPTING CREDIT CARD PAYMENTS FOR BUSINESS transactions has aided our business greatly in that we get our money almost immediately instead of extending terms and patiently waiting thirty or more days for payment. The downside is we must carefully check and verify that all transactions are legitimate before processing a credit card payment. We have had a good track record with customers paying via credit card, but that streak recently ended.

A new customer from Indonesia purchased three of our advanced direction-finding Wi-Fi tools and needed them shipped international priority via FedEx, which is extremely expensive. It seemed a bit strange, but we'd never had a problem with international credit cards before, and all his questions and e-mail correspondences seemed legitimate. A few days later, I received a call from a lawnmower shop somewhere in Minnesota. A man with a strong midwestern accent said, "Why the hell are you charging $14,000 dollars on my card? My wife is going to kill me!" I told him I had no idea what he was talking about, and he explained that three days ago our company (BVS) had charged his credit card in the amount of $14,000. I told him this was not possible because his lawnmower shop was not a customer of ours. I put him on hold as I pulled all the receipts and associated invoices for the week. As I flipped through them, the amount for the Indonesia shipment exactly matched his charge: $14,000. I then realized the Indonesian "customer" had provided me with the lawnmower shop's stolen credit card to fraudulently purchase items from BVS. This Indonesian thief was trying not only to pay with a stolen credit card but to walk away with free equipment from BVS and was clearly a snake.

The Indonesian order details rushed back to me and in that retrospective moment, it all felt "too good to be true," which, of course, it was. My father, Gary Schober (BVS founder and CTO), always said: "In business if it seems 'too good to be true,' it probably isn't good or true." His words echoed in my head and down my spine to meet the chill that ran up my back at the same instant. I asked the man on the phone to confirm the card number I read off, and it was a match. We had both been scammed, but I wondered how it had happened. I apologized profusely and told the irate midwestern lawnmower shop owner that I would contact the bank and credit card company immediately to reverse the charge. After I hung up the phone, I went back to the Indonesian customer's file and reviewed all correspondence. No red flags, other than the fact that it was all too easy. The customer accepted the price up front without asking for a discount (somewhat rare) and paid a premium for FedEx International Priority One shipping. *We've been had*, I thought to myself, and this would prove to be a painful and expensive lesson. And this was our second hack.

When I contacted BoA, they told me that they had already initiated a chargeback. A chargeback is when a cardholder (in this case, the lawnmower repair shop owner) disputes a charge with their bank and the bank reverses the payment and refunds the cardholder after an investigation. This is reasonable, but what happened to the investigation? I wasn't contacted about the fraudulent charge. BoA told me that BVS should have been more careful and that we would receive a letter within one week regarding the chargeback and investigation results. I had the right to write a rebuttal letter showing proof that charge was not fraudulent, which made no sense since I now knew our Indonesian "client" had purchased equipment with a stolen credit card.

It was troubling how quickly and without any notice that money went into and out of our account. The investigation felt one-sided, but this is common because consumers, much more than businesses, are well protected in the United States against credit-card fraud. Credit-card fraud is a form of identity theft, and federal law limits the cardholder's liability to $50 in the event of credit card theft (US Government Publishing Office: 15 U.S.C. 1643 – LIABILITY OF HOLDER OF CREDIT CARDS). In reality, if you are a victim as a consumer, your bank will most likely absorb the fraudulent charge if you provide an affidavit explaining the theft and amount stolen. There are strong laws protecting consumers who fall victim to credit card theft. The fraudulent charges are refunded quickly (as well as the fee, when investigated). It's no mystery why credit cards are so widely used and accepted in the United States.

Then, an important detail occurred to me. It would take approximately one week for the three instruments to arrive in Indonesia; perhaps I could intercept the shipment before the thief received it. This was another critical moment for me, not just because I could potentially salvage $14,000 of product from the clutches of a thief, but also because it made me realize the importance of sharing information in a timely manner. By picking up the phone when he did, that irate lawnmower shop owner thought he was giving me a piece of his mind, but what he really gave me was a fighting chance to stop the theft from completely ripping us off. Because digital transactions occur at the speed of light, you can actually save someone else from suffering the same fate, even if you don't realize you are doing it at the time.

It wasn't so much that the bank confirmed a stolen credit card was used to buy goods from our company that hurt—it was the way they nonchalantly said it literally happens every day. The bank viewed it as a cost of doing business, but I refused to make it my cost. I asked if there would be further investigation and they said most likely not, as the amount was insignificant and the credit card company and bank would eat the loss. They assured me they would assist in getting everything fixed.

I could not for the life of me accept that $14,000 in lost goods was insignificant and that this happens every day. I looked up the order's tracking information and found the shipment had not yet gone through customs in Indonesia. I then got on the phone with Federal Express and explained the entire situation. They were able to stop the shipment immediately and have it shipped back to me, which was $1,100 round trip. I had to eat the shipping charges, but I was able to get our products back and, more importantly, I was not completely ripped off by a nameless, faceless cyberthief.

If you ever encounter any of the aforementioned details, stop and do some investigation. I imagined what might have happened if I'd not gotten the phone call from the lawnmower shop guy for a few more days: The charge he noticed would have been charged back from our account, which would have been a double whammy! We would have lost the sale and the goods. More than likely, the lawnmower shop victim or his wife were shopping online, and their credit card was compromised and sold on the dark web. Their card was then purchased by the Indonesian thief, who more than likely provided the same credit card to dozens of businesses. My naivety and excitement about lucrative international business at the time fed right into the thief's trap. Since then, I have learned to always check the bank account and merchant account regularly and frequently look for anything suspicious. The Internet forces us all to opt into a global economy, whether we know it or not. That brings many opportunities, but just as many thieves, jerks, and liars.

I quickly came to learn that this technique of stealing through identity theft is common. In hindsight, a few warning signs should have alerted me. Any business owners shipping internationally should keep the following details in mind before accepting credit card payment from anyone:

They needed multiple units, large dollar purchase, paid in full via credit card

They did not negotiate a discount.

They had it shipped the fastest, most expensive way, in order to receive it before the fraudulent charge was detected.

Everything in the process seemed too good to be true. The ordeal of accepting a fraudulent credit card was troublesome and very nearly quite expensive. I have realized that although I was duped by a cyberthief, the process was a learning lesson I am determined to never go through again.

———

QUICK TIP: If you accept credit cards, be extremely cautious if your customer wants multiple items shipped in the most expedited manner, especially if internationally. STOP and ask them questions, such as the name of the issuing bank, or a photo ID to verify their credentials.

CHAPTER 3

HACKED AGAIN: TIME FOR A NEW BANK

THOSE AGGRAVATING FRADULENT CHARGES TOLD ME it was time to move our business to another financial institution. Not only had our company debit card been compromised, but shortly thereafter my personal card became compromised from the same bank. I decided to look for another bank and settled on TD Bank, partly because I was assured they had good security monitoring in place to prevent hacks and security breaches, and partly because their branch office was just down the street. I asked many technical questions of the local bank representative, such as how they prevent fraudulent transactions and handle password management. I knew nothing was one hundred percent safe, but I had a feeling of comfort with the multiple layers of security in place and a password that required changing upon login every thirty days. The bank also issued each corporate officer a key fob with a tumbling code for large wire transfers or approvals that were executed. I was careful to create a complex password and changed it routinely every thirty days as instructed. Ironically, thirty days seems to be just the right amount of time it takes me to finally digest and regurgitate a truly strong password. The thirty-day password changing policy certainly put the kibosh on my memory, but at least the bank has security in mind.

That warm-and-fuzzy, secure feeling with the new bank and all their security measures was short-lived, however, as I logged in to see well over $65,000 missing from our corporate checking account on a Monday morning in late 2013.

I frantically dialed the bank, asked for the branch manager, and told them it was an emergency. I was fairly certain our account had been hacked, and with this much money missing, I couldn't afford to wait patiently on the phone. They quickly connected me to the fraud department, which was very helpful once I proved who I was (a lengthy process involving divulging everything about myself from DNA to the present), but I understood. They needed to make sure I truly was who I said I was.

Suddenly, this bank's promise of being "America's Most Convenient Bank" held little value for me as a customer. "America's Most Secure Bank" or "America's Most Likely to Have Your Money Bank" spoke to me much more than convenience ever had.

We went through numerous transactions that had occurred within the last hour, and none had been authorized by our company. The fraud department told me they would initiate a federal investigation and froze the account so no more funds could come out without proper authorization. They did not provide details about who had taken the money when I asked. So I decided to press them a bit for more information and mentioned that I focus on cybersecurity and could not understand how anyone had access to my account when all of their layers of security were in place, and I had an obscure and very complex password that I changed monthly. They told me not to worry, and I would get all my money back. I told them that was a given, but I wanted to know the specific names of the individuals illegally debiting funds from our company account. They said they would need to put me on hold to see if they could provide that information. A few minutes later, they came back on the line to say that since I had specifically requested that information, they were required to provide it.

The largest single debit was well over $50,000 and because it was under federal investigation, I cannot disclose the exact amount or specific names in this book. What I can say is that the debit was from a woman in New Jersey who transferred it to her Chase account as a wire and noted it as a "final mortgage payment."

There were more debits and more names. I took down every name the bank disclosed to me to verify that they were not in any way associated with my company (such as a former employee, client, prospect, etc.). Then I did a few Google searches, but none of the names appeared. These were real people with real accounts, but, more than likely, their identities had been stolen, and their accounts were being used to siphon money from other accounts, such as ours.

After a long discussion with the bank's fraud department, I decided to go down to the local branch and open a new account in person. They recommended I close the other account, but I decided to leave it open awhile for monitoring purposes and wait until all the incoming wire transfers and outstanding checks had cleared. Ironically, the frozen account for which the bank had assured me could not have any further debits had three additional attempts to debit money, which I kindly brought to the attention of the fraud department. I quickly realized, in this instance, that this was not due to any lax security at my end but rather that someone with an intimate knowledge of the bank's inner workings was targeting my company.

The bank was apologetic and answered all my questions. I asked how often this happened and they sheepishly admitted "often," but that I needn't worry because I would receive every dollar back. This wasn't the first time I'd heard this standard banking line, but it still didn't do much to alleviate my worries. I was more concerned with how to prevent it from ever happening again. Bank representatives did not offer any specific insights or suggestions, other than tell us to make sure we shred all old documents with our account numbers on them. I was also told to be careful about whom I pay by check, because our account number is on the check. In other words, make sure you know all your vendors. BVS uses over a thousand different vendors throughout the course of a year so it is tough to know all of them, much less trust all of them.

For extra security and safety, the bank changed our account to one that is closely monitored on a regular basis for any suspicious activity. We still have levels of security, but the bank also internally watches the account for any suspicious activity to be able to immediately freeze the account, if needed. This combination of layers of security, bank monitoring, and my paranoid monitoring has resulted in no new compromises since then, but the other shoe can always drop.

The bank did not know all the answers but it was responsive to all my questions, to the best of its ability. The frustrating part was that, in the back of my mind, I continually asked myself if this will happen again in the future. And did I do anything wrong? The ambiguity continued to fester in my mind, and then I thought back to what people did before modern banking: they simply stockpiled cash in their mattresses. More than fifty-three percent of people keep some cash hidden in their homes. The most common place is actually the freezer. There is some level of comfort in that I am not alone.

(Kelli B. Grant, "Under a mattress, in the freezer: Why so many are hiding cash," CNBC, January 29, 2015. *http://www.cnbc.com/id/102377632).*

CHAPTER 4

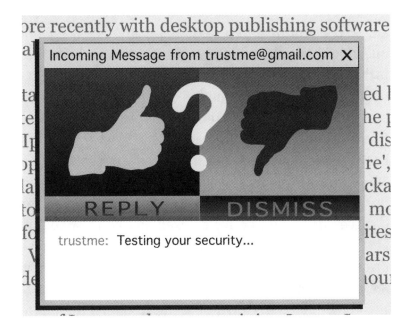

WEBSITE SECURITY TESTED

THE LIFELINE OF OUR BUSINESS is *www.bvsystems.com*. In modern business, a company's website lives in the heart of any marketing plan. Almost everything goes back to the website: the company's identity, the products or services it offers, how to buy the products, product specifications, manuals, software downloads, the online store, YouTube video links, etc. A well-designed website will directly translate to an increase in business. We continually update our BVS website with our latest wireless products, media interviews, white paper technical articles, and manuals.

About a year ago, we added a chat feature, allowing any web visitor to start a session and ask us any type of question. Typically, customers are simply curious about technology and pricing. Most of our high-end products do not have pricing information online. This is both good and bad. While there is a tremendous value in being able to talk to eager customers and steer them toward the best product solutions that meet their budgets, I hate when people try to sell me on items I do not need nor particularly want, such as extended warranties or accessories. So I do have mixed emotions, good and bad, about chat sessions when a prospect wants a quick price. I liken it to my mother-in-law driving my new Mercedes right off the cliff.

Many customers do not want to share their real contact information, and on our end we are trying to gauge just how serious (or real) the customer is. Our webmaster and media director, Craig Schober, does a brilliant job of organizing and updating a never-ending march of specifications sheets, manuals, and all manner of media-related items. He also happens to maintain all chat sessions by answering the basic questions himself and forwarding others to our sales or support teams.

Back in December 2014, he received a mysterious chat in which the prospect asked a few general questions but ended the chat session with, "I was just testing your security." Craig, realizing this well might be a hacker, called me on the intercom and said, "You better look at an e-mail I just forwarded to you. Someone is making vague threats by saying they are testing our security." I quickly reviewed the chat session but was unfamiliar with the character's name or IP address. My first instinct was to do a few Google searches, but nothing popped up or seemed out of the ordinary.

This suspicious chat claimed to be "testing" our website security.

Then I remembered my conversation a few days earlier with some colleagues in Israel who developed some incredible analytical software that crawls the deep, dark web and performs some quick queries on individuals and topics that might lead to a cyberhack. In a sense, they developed an early threat-detection engine—not unlike the Tom Cruise movie *Minority Report*, but for cyberattacks. I gathered the evidence from the suspicious chat session, packaged it up in an e-mail, and asked them to do some background checking on the possible cyberhacker testing our website security. Sure enough, they come back with sufficient information to convince me that the chat-session initiator was, in fact, a legitimate notorious hacker up to no good. Naturally, I started to wonder if we were going to be hacked again. Now what might the hacker attempt—a DDoS attack on our website so we couldn't take orders through our online store, or something worse? A DDoS (distributed denial of service) is a type of attack that prevents or impairs the authorized use of information-system resources or services by which a targeted website is flooded with garbage so it can no longer operate, and business is disrupted for a period of time.

I thought back to some of the most recent interviews I had given on Bloomberg TV and Al Jazeera America and and wondered if this character decided I posed a threat in some way. I scanned variations of their chat handle through all of my LinkedIn contacts, but no hits there. Next, I put the e-mail through a search of 200,000+ e-mails from the past decade (and yes, I do back them up regularly, but not to the cloud) but nothing suspicious popped up. I remembered some research I was doing recently on social media and how cyberhackers thrive in this space, especially for bragging rights. So I jumped on my personal and company Twitter accounts to conduct a search and immediately found something: this cyberhacker was following both my @BVSystems and @ScottBVS Twitter accounts, so I blocked them both just to be safe.

I always stress to business colleagues the importance of vetting who you allow to follow you on the social media channels. If you allow hackers to actively follow you and your company and, at the same time, you are providing tips and best practices on how *not* to be a hacking victim, you may have just drawn a target on your   back. We immediately changed the passwords for our website and all of the associated e-mail accounts. We even notified Shopify, our online store provider, and updated all associated passwords. We noted web outages over the course of several weeks; since our web host reported no specific problems with their servers at that time, we knew the hackers were targeting our website with repeated DDoS attacks.

We reported the website downtimes to our host, and the company was able to closely analyze normal customer traffic to our website to distinguish this traffic from the sharp spikes often attributed to DDoS attacks. Since DDoS attacks consume a considerable amount of bandwidth, the ISP/host provider will want to address the problem quickly so the attack does not affect its customer base. They are likely to "null route" your traffic, which results in dropping network packets of user data destined for your web server before they arrive. A null route is a network route that goes nowhere. Matching data packets are dropped and basically ignored rather than forwarded, acting as a kind of very limited firewall to mitigate large-scale DDoS attacks. Since this is costly to your host provider—and, more than likely, *your* business—you need to take swift action. In some cases, if the DDoS attack is massive, you may need to consult a professional firm specializing in countering DDoS attacks, such as VeriSign.

QUICK TIP: If you notice your website is not operating normally—perhaps it's running extremely slow—immediately report this to your Internet Service Provider (ISP) or host provider. You may be the victim of a DDoS attack.

CHAPTER 5

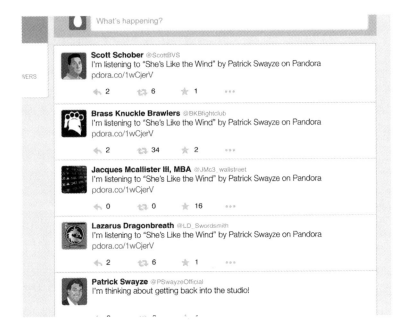

What's happening?

Scott Schober @ScottBVS
I'm listening to "She's Like the Wind" by Patrick Swayze on Pandora
pdora.co/1wCjerV
↩ 2   ⇄ 6   ★ 1   ...

Brass Knuckle Brawlers @BKBfightclub
I'm listening to "She's Like the Wind" by Patrick Swayze on Pandora
pdora.co/1wCjerV
↩ 2   ⇄ 34   ★ 2   ...

Jacques Mcallister III, MBA @JMc3_wallstreet
I'm listening to "She's Like the Wind" by Patrick Swayze on Pandora
pdora.co/1wCjerV
↩ 0   ⇄ 0   ★ 16   ...

Lazarus Dragonbreath @LD_Swordsmith
I'm listening to "She's Like the Wind" by Patrick Swayze on Pandora
pdora.co/1wCjerV
↩ 2   ⇄ 6   ★ 1   ...

Patrick Swayze @PSwayzeOfficial
I'm thinking about getting back into the studio!

TWITTER TARGETED

ON JANUARY 1, 2015, I CHECKED MY BUSINESS E-MAIL and noticed had some new Twitter followers on my @ScottBVS account. This Twitter account I personally manage for my business, so I like to carefully check profiles before following anyone in return. Say what you want about the haters and noise on Twitter, it continues to connect us with a large audience we otherwise might not reach. At the same time, there is propensity for a lot of whackos out there to misuse Twitter. That morning, I saw a very strange tweet on my Twitter timeline that I did not write.

"Hacked again!" I exclaimed as my seven-year-old son peered over my shoulder.

"Was it the Lizard Squad? You better watch your tail, Dad," he said.

I had to laugh. He had picked up bits and pieces from my TV interviews about the Sony hacks and the notorious international hacking group the Lizard Squad, which is mainly known for claiming DDoS attacks that disrupted online video-gaming services in 2014. One notorious Lizard Squad member was convicted of 50,700 counts of cybercrime. More on the Lizard Squad later.

At the time, I was enjoying our winter break up at the cabin, thinking about the successful year we just completed and anticipating a very busy 2015. We had a tremendous backlog of orders to fulfill when we came back from break. In our online store, we continue to sell our popular security tools 24–7, so being closed for twelve days over winter break is a bit stressful; we are accumulating new orders we cannot fulfill until we are back at work and in production.

The hack appeared to be a share from Pandora, as if I were listening to a song and wanted to share it with my contacts on Twitter. I quickly discounted this, as I hadn't listened to Pandora that week. The second tell was that it was a Patrick Swayze song; I don't listen to any of his music, so I shared it with Craig to make sure he was not playing a joke on me, but he thought I had tweeted it. After some searching on the Internet, I learned other people had their Twitter accounts hacked with the exact same message. It might have been a victimless crime, but I immediately changed my Twitter password and the Patrick Swayze tweets have not returned since.

We investigated and found that it is a common hacker practice to hack Twitter accounts. Many cyberthieves will obtain a Twitter password, change it, and then take over the account by tweeting out links to ads or malicious websites. Fortunately, I caught the fake @ScottBVS Tweet early and deleted it just before changing my password again. @ScottBVS is used to keep our customers and other interested parties up to date on my TV appearances and cybersecurity safety tips, and there I was: hacked again.

Upon further investigation, I noticed that @Anonymous was among my Twitter followers. Anonymous is a group of "hacktivist" entities known for well-publicized publicity stunts and DDoS attacks against government, religious, and corporate websites like ours. An image commonly associated with Anonymous is a man wearing a mask, representing leaderless organization and anonymity. By the end of 2014, I was weighing in on many of the Xbox Live hacks, and Anonymous sent me a tweet that said, "We didn't hack XBOX Live/PSN

@LizardMafia did." Anonymous eventually took out the Lizard Squad, who, as mentioned earlier, used DDoS attacks primarily to disrupt gaming-related services. Anonymous gave them a taste of their own medicine by delivering a DDoS attack on their website. I also found @LizardMafia (clearly the Lizard Squad) as a follower to my Twitter account. Since I was reporting in on both of these hacker organizations, they began following my tweets and reports, which is somewhat flattering in that circle.

I deal in high-profile cybersecurity stories every day. I research them, speak on the topic, and offer security insights to help individuals and organizations deal with security breaches. Since they all come to me in the form of headlines or stories, I never really get to solve the mysteries or find out just whodunit. They are not my stories, so why should I expect any kind of personal closure? But since 2012, I have been personally faced with my own hacking scandals that involved my company's banks, stolen money, compromised credit cards, and unknown thieves who are probably still out there.

When I was about eleven, my brother and I had our new Huffy bikes stolen from our driveway in broad daylight. As someone who loved riding bikes everyday after school, I not only felt violated but also devastated. The police were called, but a solid lead never turned up. There is something particularly unnerving when a cyber-hacker steals money from your checking account, and you never fully come to terms with how it happened and whether the thief was ever brought to justice. I'm now certain that I will never have full closure. Bank fraud resulting in over $65,000 in stolen funds and two stolen Huffy bikes might not be the same crime monetarily, but they were emotionally devastating to both the eleven-year-old Scott Schober, as well as the forty-four-year-old CEO of a small business and cybersecurity expert, Scott N. Schober.

QUICK TIP: Scan your social media followers often . . . you never know when they may be gathering information to hack you.

PART 2

LESSONS LEARNED:
HOW TO PROTECT YOURSELF

CHAPTER 6

LOCKPICKING THE BRAIN

WHEN ANALYZING SECURITY BREACHES, a common element many neglect to consider is the human element. Hackers can be extremely patient, waiting for victims to let down their guard. This can come at any time: during a chat session, a late-night e-mail response, a frantic text message. We are connected to each other 24–7, so the potential is ever present to be tricked or coerced into giving away valuable information. One of the most effective ways to gain instant access to valuable personal and secure information is through passwords. According to the 2013 *Data Breach Investigations Report (DBIR)* compiled yearly by Verizon's risk team, approximately seventy-six percent of attacks on corporate networks involved weak passwords. This further underscores the importance of strong passwords.

All Internet users are forced to memorize passwords, user names, and security challenge questions that might be easy to remember but, unfortunately, that same memory convenience also makes them easy to hack. Hackers are sometimes likened to thieves with lock picks. They have certain skills, and once they can pick the lock to your front door, they have access to all of your belongings. This is a misconception, though, because while hackers do have skills, the only thing they're looking to pick is your brain. And once they gain access to your brain, they can access everything you own and what you know too. They do this not by picking your lock but by stealing your very own key. Passwords are like memory keys that only you know, but they can be stolen by anyone in the world looking in the right places for the right clues.

By picking your brain, hackers gain access to much more than could ever fit in your physical home or office. Hackers are like detectives scraping for social, family, and professional clues from websites, e-mails, texts, and, of course, the old garbage can. These clues appear innocuous enough when separated by miles, jobs, or IP addresses, but when pieced together, hackers can resolve passwords that were previously unguessable even by supercomputer standards. Then, if this same password has been used for multiple accounts or websites, a victim's entire online world can tumble down like dominoes. From there, it's only a matter of minutes before the World Wide Web meets the real world, and real money and real private information is stolen or sold off. This can all spawn from a single act of human weakness—trust.

People share information with others they do not even know every single day. Perhaps a phone call comes into a corporation and the receptionist answers. She is asked for the wireless password for the company's Wi-Fi network so someone can send an urgent document to the CEO. If the caller sounds convincing enough, the receptionist may disclose the password without a second thought to what she just divulged. Hackers often prey on attributes of human emotion, such as greed or compassion, resulting in innocent people being victimized.

A good example springs to mind when I think of my grandparents. They were in their upper eighties at the time and residing in an assisted living facility with approximately 1,500 elderly individuals. My grandfather answered the phone one day and heard, "Grandpa, it's me. I am in trouble and up in Canada."

Grandpa responded, "Who is this?"

The caller said, 'It's me, your grandchild."

He said, "Brian, is that you?"

"Yes, I need help. I drove up to Canada with some friends and they had drugs in the car and we all got arrested."

Grandpa said, "Oh no, you need to be careful who you associate with."

The hacker responded, "I need you to send me $10,000 immediately, and they will drop all charges and let me out of jail."

"OK, how do I do that?" asked my grandfather.

"Go quickly to the nearest Staples store, get a wire transfer document, and transfer the funds to this account number [one he gave] at your bank immediately. But don't wait, because if you don't do it now, they will keep me locked up all weekend and might not even drop the charges. And whatever you do, don't tell my mom."

Grandpa grabbed Grandma and explained what happened as they raced across the street to Staples to find the wire transfer document template. As they were waiting in line filling out the information, a cashier over-hears them talking. She asked, "Do you mind me asking to whom are you trying to wire transfer funds?" They told her about their grandson's call and all the details of his story. The cashier told them to wait there because several other people had come into the store that very day with the same story. My grandparents agreed to call Brian to be sure, and he answered. They realized he was not in Canada *or* in jail, but rather down in Georgia. All was fine, but they nearly lost $10,000.

The hackers preyed upon my grandfather's emotions and sounded convincing enough over the phone. It is important to remember that hackers come in many forms. Over the phone, they are good actors. In an e-mail, they supply a good story with a link just waiting to be clicked. On social networks, they can be multiple people talking to you at the same time. Whatever form they come in, they always choose to engage with the easiest targets. Elderly or naive victims make for the best targets. This is wrong, yet happens every single day. If someone you do not know asks you for money or help, they are probably targeting you.

Question everything, and don't be afraid to do some quick research to see if the claims are indeed factual. The hackers are probably online looking at your profile while they are on the phone with you, so there's no reason you cannot do the same to verify they are who they say they are. If my grandfather was able to test the validity during the phone call by interjecting a question like, "Where are you, so I can come and pick you up?" it may have resulted in the hacker hanging up and trying someone else. There are no risk-free propositions when dealing with unknown individuals. The best thing to do is guard ourselves enough so hackers leave us alone and target someone else.

The more I learn about hackers and their techniques, the more disgusted I am by them. I have decided to make it my goal to share my story and best practices in hopes those listening will take some preventative measures so they do not become just another cyberattack statistic.

Quick Tip: Be careful whom you share your Wi-Fi password with. If you have shared your password with anyone, change your password to a stronger one immediately after that person leaves.

CHAPTER 7

BEWARE OF THE "WARES"

MALWARE IS MALICIOUS SOFTWARE USED TO DISRUPT normal computer operations, gather information, and potentially even gain access to private computer systems. The term "malware" is somewhat general in that there are a variety of intrusive, specialized software techniques that hackers use, including ransomware, spyware, scareware, worms, Trojan horses, and computer viruses. When the first computer worms showed up, they were simply experiments or even pranks. Contrast that to today's malware, and we see a clear progression with destructive results for individuals, companies, and even governments. Hackers use focused malware attacks against individuals to acquire banking statements, credit card numbers, and passwords to unlock even more personal data.

Over time, malware has evolved into software designed by coders allowing hackers to profit. Some malware takes over an individual's computer for a particular illicit purpose, such as sending child pornography or to have an infected computer engage in a DDoS attack, as was recently inflicted on Microsoft's Xbox Live and Sony's PlayStation network gaming services. This devastating attack affected well over one hundred million upset gamers eager to delve into their newly gifted Christmas games and consoles. The Lizard Squad hacking group took credit for this enormous attack (much more on this in the later chapter regarding the Sony hacks).

Cybercriminals continue to improve the quality of malware hacks, but some of the initial attacks were rather crude. Poor grammar or broken image links made it evident to most people that they were amateurs. Things have certainly changed, as now cyberhackers use advanced toolkits to build convincing e-mail malware that looks legitimate. These toolkits can be purchased in the underground dark web, allowing the cyberthief to target a website and scrape particular information, such as logos and the specific language. Therefore, consumers need to be ever more wary when receiving e-mails with attachments.

A particularly sneaky variant of malware is called spyware, which, as the name implies, is designed to "spy on" (or monitor) a user's web-browsing habits and insert unsolicited pop-up advertisements—or even redirect them to another site for shady marketing purposes. There are big dollars in this area, so unsavory organizations are all too happy to place spyware on unsuspecting users' computers. The actual spyware is not spread like a virus, but, rather, is installed through a security hole discovered on a vulnerable computer, often inadvertently by the victims themselves.

Ransomware is one of the scariest emerging forms of malware: Cybercriminals will install ransomware on your computer so they can effectively lock your computer from a remote location. Ransomware demands payment in exchange for a key and threatens users with further consequences for not complying. Many cyberthugs demand Bitcoins as payment, which is an anonymous form of digital currency that cannot be easily traced or tied to an individual. Bitcoin as digital currency is an exciting concept, but is predominantly connected with cybercriminals masking their identities and Internet tracks. A typical example involves ransomware infecting your computer in order for hackers to steal particularly valuable files. Knowing you have valuable data, they demand payment to reverse the damage or release the files back to you. If you do not pay, they sell the contents to the highest bidder or sometimes just post it on public blogs. And sometimes they do not even need to steal any files, but rather, just encrypt all the files residing on your computer's hard drive.

Unless you meet their demands, they will leave the encrypted files (now worthless without the key) with you.

Many people assume a cybercriminal has to have physical access in order to install malware on a computer. This is rarely the case, because it's much easier to let the victims install it themselves by clicking on malicious links embedded in harmless-looking e-mail messages. Some ransomware is placed as a direct result of the user clicking on an instant message that pops up on the computer screen or by visiting a particular social networking site and clicking on a pop-up login request. Be cautious of the websites you visit, because some will immediately download malicious software to your computer. Apply best practices by avoiding unfamiliar websites and pop-ups, as these attacks are directed toward the curious and naive.

Ransomware has been a problem for many years, but it's only recently started showing up on mobile devices such as smart phones. When you activate the program or an app, it blocks you from accessing the data on the device and displays a message demanding payment by untraceable methods like Bitcoin or Money-Pak. On mobile devices, ransomware usually spreads via e-mail, from visiting malicious websites that host pornography or by installing pirated apps. And malware developers have only gotten smarter. Some ransomware apps can now spread via text messages. When a device is infected, the malicious app will send an SMS to everyone on the device's contact list with a message designed to trick the recipients into clicking on a link. SMS stands for Short Message Service, which is a texting messaging service used on mobile communication devices. When the readers open the link, they are directed to install the malware on their devices, thus repeating the process with a new round of victims.

Typically, consumers are encouraged to back up their critical data in the event it is compromised or lost. As storage costs continually go down, the shift toward backing up to the cloud will continue to be the norm. I back up my computer locally every day because you never know when your computer might be compromised or you need to fall back to that vital backup. Smartphone users back up their phones to the cloud or plug into their PC to perform a routine backup. Of course, some of the new ransomware strains target stored login information for the cloud backup services, which will have the capability to lock up those files, as well. It is important to be vigilant and back up your hard drive regularly. Store the backup data at a remote location, so you are not the next victim.

When corporations face a malicious software attack via some form of ransomware, many quickly cave and pay the requested ransom just to get back to business. Since time is money, they figure it's just another cost of doing business, and they can save money by paying the ransom to save some time. Perhaps they don't have a choice, and the only existing copy has been stolen or hopelessly encrypted. But since backups have become a regular part of life in the modern world, more often businesses do have backup copies but do not want to take the time and resources to file a request to their IT department and wait around for the backups to get them up to speed again. But just as credit card fraud, chargebacks, and stolen plastic have become the cost of doing business for some in the past few decades, it doesn't mean we have to write off ransomware as just another cost in this digital age.

Many people ask me if they should pay ransomware if their device gets infected and hijacked. Nine times out of ten, I tell them *not* to pay the ransom. If you do send money, it rewards the criminals and there are no guarantees you'll get your information back anyway. In fact, you may simply be funding more criminal activity and emboldening the hackers. Cyberhackers might be dealing with an exchange of money for services, but that does not make them business people. They are lying criminals, first and foremost. Can you really trust them to provide the key to unlock your data? They will try to convince you that they are just like any other business and need you as a customer, as if customer service is something they truly value. Do not fall for that twisted logic and delusions of customer relations. Ignore them or work with the authorities to catch them. Anything else ensures a longer-term relationship with you playing the role of the victim every time.

In 2014, the Android OS was a prime target for emerging mobile device ransomware attacks. One such example was called "Koler.A," which would lock up the device's screen when visiting certain pornographic websites. From the moment of infection, a worm variant called "Worm.Koler" would send an SMS message to all of the user's contacts from the mobile phone's address book. Each contact received an SMS text message stating that someone created a profile using his or her

BEWARE OF THE "WARES" 45

photos with a link. If the unsuspecting recipient clicked on the link, they were taken to a Dropbox page with a download for an application called Photo viewer. When the Photo viewer application was installed, it would pop up a ransom message demanding payment of $300 to unlock the device containing illicit content. Many victims got scared and quickly paid the ransom without thinking it through or even weighing their options.

If you believe you are the victim of a ransomware attack on your Android mobile device, try to immediately reboot the device into the safe mode. Just like a computer, safe mode boots the Android device with just the bare minimum operating system. This prevents malicious software from running at startup and allows you to safely remove it. The instructions on activating safe mode vary from device to device, so check the manual and the manufacturer's web page for specific instructions. Once you have access to the operating system, you can uninstall the malware or run an antivirus app that will remove it for you.

How do you prevent malware from attacking your Android device in the first place? Think before you click. Hackers will make the link look appealing and legitimate, but do not click on any links you were not expecting in e-mails or text messages. If the message comes from someone you know but weren't expecting a message from, think about contacting the person before opening the link. A quick phone call may save you much stress. Make sure the "Unknown Sources" check box in your smartphone's security settings is left blank. This option is usually disabled by default, but sometimes users enable it to side-load legitimate apps that are not available from Google Play Store and forget to uncheck it after they finish. The location can vary, but it is usually found under Settings > Security.

Keep backups of your local data. With many apps, data is stored on a remote server, not your device. When you open the app, it downloads the necessary information through your data connection. If you have applications that store data on the device or memory card, make sure to keep a backup of the information on your computer. For rooted Android devices there are applications that will create an image of everything on the device and save it in a file you can transfer to your computer or upload to cloud storage.

Cybercriminals tend to focus malicious ransomware attacks on older operating systems that are no longer supported or have out-of-date security patches or certificates. These systems include older variants of Windows that receive little to no attention from Microsoft anymore. Consumers who are too lazy or can't justify paying for a more modern computer and current OS that includes the latest security patches are extremely vulnerable to malicious attacks. CryptoLocker was a popular ransomware program that many cyberhackers regularly used. Eventually, the program was taken down, but not without spawning a successor. CryptoWall 2.0 was introduced with more advanced features, allowing it to be concealed from detection before an attack. Crazy as it sounds, there is even a reactive support team in place to provide guidance to victims in order to simplify ransomware payments via Bitcoin.

Sometimes timing is everything. I received a request to do a radio interview about ransomware on *The Diane Rehm Show* on NPR radio in Washington, DC. I am a regular NPR listener and tune back and forth between NPR and Bloomberg radio during my daily commute. NPR beams with journalistic integrity, providing the most comprehensive news and coverage for their listeners. Ransomware is a hot topic in my world and has begun spilling over into other sectors, so NPR was looking for a comprehensive segment with experts to detail the perils and pitfalls of ransomware. A special cybersecurity edition of *The Diane Rehm Show* was to be an hour long with guest host Steve Roberts. Steve is an exceptional host and his longtime wife, Cokie Roberts, was a familiar voice of network TV and is now on NPR.

I completed the pre-interview, and they mentioned that I would be on live with cybersecurity expert Cheri McGuire from Symantec and a Tennessee sheriff who had been a victim of ransomware. They asked if I knew of another expert in ransomware and a name immediately popped into my head. I had just finished reading *Spam Nation*, a fascinating account of the international spamming business. The author was Brian Krebs, a former *Washington Post* reporter who now ran his own cybersecurity blog. I couldn't think of anyone more knowledgeable on current ransomware scams or malware in general, so I suggested they give Brian a call. A few days later, they got back to me with a confirmation on the interview date and said Brian had agreed to join the panel discussion, too.

The interview itself went great, and we even had the

opportunity to respond to some live calls toward the end. They set up a webpage just for this interview segment on the NPR website. I read through some of the comments; there were several hundred within the first twenty-four hours. Now it's up to the NPR listeners; I hope they implement some of the recommendations we made to strengthen their cyber defenses. I want to hear from everyone, but it's a little discouraging when all the comments involve victimization and theft. Prevention is always the key, so when I hear from small business owners, consumers, and even friends who have implemented my recommendations, I am nothing but smiles.

CYBER STAT: Ransomware malware is sold on the dark web black-market websites for as little as $60 per program, so the entry point to becoming a cyberthief is very low.

Brian Krebs and Scott Schober appear on NPR's The Diane Rehm Show *discussing Ransomware: The Latest Cybersecurity Threat.*

Hackers have come up with some novel means to defraud companies that advertise online by developing malware called "click fraud." Internet advertising payments are typically only counted when an individual clicks on a particular ad (called pay-per-click or PPC), and the advertiser is then charged by the number of clicks. Click fraud means bogus clicks were tallied for ads that were never viewed at all and can occur when a person manually clicks on the fraudulent advertising hyperlinks. Hackers took this concept to the next step, though, by developing automated software and even utilizing online "bots" programmed to click these banner ads and pay-per-click (PPC) ad links. Adware can be covertly installed on computers through either users being tricked into clicking a malware link, or users employing a file-sharing program to install freeware that secretly includes adware.

There are estimates that over twenty percent of ad clicks are the result of click fraud, which represents countless millions of dollars advertisers are spending with no benefit. I brought this up at one of our weekly marketing meetings, and it certainly gave me pause. To think of all the thousands we spend on Internet advertising and that we might be throwing as much as twenty percent of that money in the garbage is sickening.

When I talk to others about malware, I try to help people appreciate that it is about more than just money. Malware is about destruction and chaos. A well-known example is Stuxnet, which was a notorious computer worm discovered in 2010. This malware worm was specifically designed to attack programmable logic controllers (PLCs) for industries that control machinery or assembly lines. This particular story caught my attention because my company has many customers using PLCs. PLCs can be used in centrifuges, which can be used to separate nuclear waste. Stuxnet sought out specific software on computer networks running Microsoft Windows operating systems. The Stuxnet worm would initially be introduced through a common USB flash drive, and once installed on the target computer, it would modify the codes that specifically controlled valves and motors, resulting in strange and unexpected instructions sent to the PLC— yet would appear as normal values to the user. Stuxnet is believed to have been the cause of destruction specifically controlled valves and motors, resulting in strange and unexpected instructions sent to the PLC—yet would appear as normal values to the user. Stuxnet is believed to have been the cause of destruction for twenty percent of Iran's uranium enrichment infrastructure.

Brian Krebs first reported on the Stuxnet worm back in July 2010. It appears that almost sixty percent of the infected computers targeted were in Iran. The Stuxnet worm was carefully designed to infect only three other computers and then erase itself. All the research to date seems to identify the Stuxnet worm was designed by the United States specifically to target Iranian centrifuge structures. Focused attacks such as Stuxnet are not the work of an amateur, but rather carefully, well-placed malware by a sophisticated group. It is believed the Stuxnet worm forced a change in the centrifuge's rotor speed, raising it to a very high RPM and then to a very low RPM, thereby destroying much of the centrifuge. The evidence reported points to the United States working jointly with Israel to develop the Stuxnet worm and is considered to be one of the first ever cyberwar attacks.

QUICK TIPS:
1) Never click on any attachment or link in an e-mail sent to you, no matter how legitimate it might look.
2) DON'T pay ransom to a cyberhacker.
3) Make frequent backups in case you are ever a victim of ransomware, and make sure you physically remove the backup drive from the PC.

CHAPTER 8

IDENTITY THEFT

SOCIAL MEDIA IS BECOMING THE NORMAL MEANS of communication in most of our lives, but far too many people put too much information out there for prying eyes to gather. If you are going away on vacation, never post on Facebook or Twitter that you are going on vacation to Disney World, for example, much less the specific dates you will be there. Cyberthieves scour the Internet looking for clues to move in and hack your wireless network—even sell this information on the underground market to real-world thieves who will rob your house blind while you are relaxing poolside just outside Mickey's castle without a care in the world.

Statistics show that those who put out an abundance of personal information on social media sites are twice as likely to be victims of identity theft. According to the Federal Trade Commission (FTC), the number one consumer complaint in the United States is identity theft, putting it at the top of the list for fifteen consecutive years. What makes identify theft so easy is that people are too social. In fact, according to *whatissocialmedia.com*, thirty-five percent of Americans check in or tweet about their whereabouts on a regular basis, and fifteen percent of Americans announce to their friends when they are not home. One of the most troubling statistics is that forty percent of Americans post details of an upcoming vacation on social media sites.

At a recent cybersecurity conference, I was discussing how easy it was to socially engineer an attack and decided to use my audience as an example target. I always strive to provide examples and illustrations that an audience will connect with so they can take better steps to ultimately protect themselves. The prior day of the conference, I met many attendees and we chatted over hors d'oeuvres and drinks as we exchanged business cards. I put on my "white hat" (meaning I was going to be a benign hacker) that evening before my presentation in order to contact several innocent people I could use during my presentation. In less than one hour I was able to connect with several attendees through LinkedIn. My goal was to pretend I was a cyberhacker who was accumulating data for identity theft. I approached this in an ethical way, of course, and only to share that many people put out too much information about themselves, especially on social media.

During my presentation I briefly shared some findings with my audience of cybersecurity experts, who ranged from professors to business owners to government officials and even some students studying cybersecurity. From the initial exchange of their business cards I got the basics that anyone could typically get from a Google search: first and last name, company address, phone, fax, mobile, Twitter handle.

From there, I went to my LinkedIn profile and invited them to connect with me. Since I had just met them that day and was presenting the following day, it gave me the LinkedIn credibility I needed. As soon as they connected with me, I checked to see if they viewed my profile. This is always a good indicator as to whether they have done their research. I find the vast majority of people connect with an individual without even first looking at their profile, which is problematic.

I dug into their contact information for crumbs they unknowingly put out for cyberthieves to nibble on. The first few profiles I reviewed contained full birth dates posted publicly. Why would anyone need or want to do this? Do they really enjoy the automated birthday wishes sent to them that much? If you must have every friend of yours on a social network wishing you a happy birthday, at least lie about the day and the month for security reasons. I understand if you already lie about the year. Everyone can opt out of having their birth date posted, or they can at least limit it to the year they were born. Any cyberthief armed with this information is one step closer to stealing and subsequently selling your identity. I see many folks list both their work and personal websites in one place. This provides a treasure trove of useful information to any hacker or thief because it makes focused, personal information about the individual easily available. It's like saving the step of hiring a private detective to spy on your subjects because they have already done the work for you.

Sure enough, in my little fact-finding mission, I discovered the high school attended by one individual and a picture of their pet complete with name. Here are two more valuable pieces of information that can be used as possible answers to security challenge questions. So now that I know the town where they attended high school, I can check on *Zillow.com* to find a home address in the event they did not move out of the town (in the United States, approximately one-third of people do not move from their hometowns). As I dig deeper, I gather additional clues used in hacking passwords by visiting their Facebook pages, Instagram accounts, and a few of their YouTube videos. Some searches even pull up items they had on sale in craigslist.org.

The next day, when I mention in my presentation that many of us make too much information public about our families and ourselves, I got familiar looks from everyone. We have all heard this before. But then I made it personal by asking, "Who made their birth date viewable on their LinkedIn profile?" Interestingly, no one responds. Some are too embarrassed to admit it, and some just do not remember how they configured their profile and settings. I mentioned that in under an hour, I found that roughly ten percent of the audience had their full birth dates posted. This got everyone's attention. I went on to reveal the plethora of information I gathered, assuring them I was not looking to hack them but just wanted to drive the point home.

Security is everyone's business, and we need to be careful what we put out there for anyone to see. The message was received loud and clear because after my presentation, I had numerous people come up to thank me and also to tell me they were embarrassed. When people realize they are making it too easy for hackers, they first feel a sense of shame but then a sense of relief because they know they must rein in their activity to control their fate. They are no longer helpless victims who could be hacked at any moment.

CYBER STAT: According to the Federal Trade Commission (FTC), the number one consumer complaint at the beginning of 2015 was identity theft.

When cyberthieves begin searching, they only need a few key pieces of information to fully steal your identity, most of which is easily obtained on the Internet: name, address, birth date, mother's maiden name, pet's name, high school attended, etc. When we put this information on social media, we are handing strangers the keys to our front door. Once cyberthieves obtain enough information on you, they can take out a credit card in your name and go on a shopping spree, leaving you with a mess of bills and damaged credit.

CYBER STAT: The *2015 Identity Fraud* report released by Javelin Strategy & Research reveals that fraudsters stole $16 billion from 12.7 million US consumers in 2014. Every two seconds, a new person becomes a victim of identity fraud. *www.javelinstrategy.com/brochure/347*

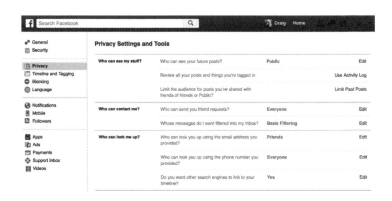

Facebook offers many privacy and security settings. Finding this menu and adjusting the settings to best protect your personal information is the real challenge.

Social media sites offer a tremendous amount of value for your upfront costs. We can all stay connected to our friends and distant loved ones for free, but there is always a cost. Make sure to know the few best practices you should implement if you plan to maintain a social presence on sites such as Facebook, Twitter, Instagram, Snapchat, and LinkedIn.

For example, set your privacy settings to the highest level, and do not share detailed facts or anything that might be an actual answer to one of your security challenge questions on any social site. In fact, try *not* to answer the security questions honestly or sensibly. The truth can actually harm you here because by answering truthfully, you are confirming other public information about you and allowing anyone to begin to assume your identity. Now if you answer the security questions with lies, gibberish, or passwords, you essentially lock out anyone trying to hack you through your security questions. The only trick is remembering your answers.

It is ironic that one of the core strengths and attractions of social media—sharing and connecting with anyone freely—is also its Achilles heel. The general rule of thumb is that the more open a social system is, the more incidents of abuse and theft will occur. These thefts or infractions don't go unchecked, but they do necessitate stronger locks and more keys. And this, in turn, can lead to user apathy or confusion. And so the vicious cycle continues because users have become accustomed to doing just enough, until inconvenience trumps usability.

One of the most popular ways cyberhackers attempt to steal your identity is by sending you an e-mail with traps and e-mail phishing scams that you can thwart by simply avoiding them. But we cannot completely avoid everything if we wish to maintain some degree of online presence. One crucial element is having a strong password, which I will talk about in later chapters.

―――――――――

QUICK TIP: Social media is beneficial, but think before you put out personal information on any social media site or you might end up being a victim of identity theft.

CHAPTER 9

CANNED SPAM

IF YOU ARE LIKE ME, YOU'RE PROBABLY WONDERING what exactly the word "spam" means and where it came from. Spam is a brand of precooked canned meat that was introduced back in 1937 by the Hormel Foods Corporation, Inc. It first became popular internationally during World War II. The 1970s *Monty Python* sketch, in which every item on a café menu contains Spam, caught on with early '80s computer users. People would send the following types of text across the screen to get unwanted users out of chat sessions or a particular screen:

SPAMSPAMSPAMSPAMSPAMSPAMSPAMSPAMSPAMSPAMSPAM

This practice was initially called flooding or trapping, but, eventually, spamming or spam became the term that stuck. Spam is annoying and often trivial but is also an effective means to dispense or spread computer viruses, Trojan horses, or malicious software. Spam exploits the innocence or naiveté of computer users. Many people ask a common question about spam: "Should I click on 'remove me,' 'opt out,' or 'unsubscribe' at the bottom of most spam e-mails?"

First you must appreciate that spammers are liars first and marketers second. They will not remove you from any lists because it does not benefit them in any way to do so. You would like to think that when you ask to be removed it happens; however, doing that actually tells the spammer you have a real e-mail address that you use. This is e-mail gold to a spammer because they can now sell your name to other spammers or add you to a list of prospects for themselves. So trying to remove yourself from a spammer's list will only guarantee you will get more spam. The best way to handle spam is to either mark it as junk mail or blacklist it.

Typical junk mail filters are a little more forgiving than blacklisting. They use algorithms to predict and confirm unsolicited e-mails in a variety of ways. Sometimes they recognize spam just from the subject heading, sometimes from the sender, and sometimes from more subtle cues like the size or file type of the attachment. In any case, they are not foolproof and are always learning as spammers adjust and change their own methods. Blacklisting is a more severe outcome. When you blacklist an e-mail, you are telling your e-mail server that you never want to see an e-mail from that sender again, no matter what. There's no going back, unless of course you move that sender into your whitelist. However, whitelisting is not ideal either, as e-mail senders can be spoofed. Ever received an e-mail from a close friend or family member that you know they didn't send? That's spam and if you were to whitelist it, you're telling your e-mail server that this contact is OK even if they are a spammer you don't want to ever hear from again. But that's the ongoing battle for our inboxes in a nutshell.

I have several e-mail accounts I use throughout the day and find I receive an average of 600 to 800 junk e-mails daily. In fact, the average person who receives twenty or more legitimate e-mails a day, will get up to 200 spam e-mails alongside the ones they open and read. That's a 1,000 percent spam rate and, when added cumulatively over a month or year, spam can result in many hours of wasted time. Certainly spam is a nuisance, but it has true costs associated to mail servers that have to receive and process it. Companies also pay expensive and highly trained IT employees to run and maintain those servers because the more spam that passes through them, the less legitimate e-mail can be delivered in a timely manner. And then there is the problem of "false positives" and "false negatives." Spam can easily be confused for legitimate e-mail. In the end, both the servers and the recipients have their personal time and resources wasted.

Spam started out as a means to market unsolicited products by sending the same e-mail to the recipient over and over. Did you ever find yourself asking if you should buy one of those flexible retracting hoses for your house? If so, then you probably have received so much spam that you start thinking you actually *need* a genuine flexible retracting hose. Yet in the past few years, spam has taken on a different form, one of criminal activity. Remember that authors of a spam e-mail are anonymous, so they can make any claims or offers they want without repercussions. That is not honest marketing, much less anyone you would ever want to do business with.

One of the largest customers for spammers are the virus writers. When a new virus is created by a cybercriminal, there needs to be an effective way to propagate the virus and often they turn to spammers and their massive lists of victims for a transmission method. Of course, the moment someone receives a spam e-mail and clicks on an attachment, it infects their computer with a malicious virus. At the end of the day, spam is more than a nuisance and actually costs tens of billions of dollars that e-mail users end up paying in the form of higher fees to service providers or lost time and productivity. If you are like me, you would probably prefer eating the real Spam in a can rather than spending many wasted hours each week sorting through e-mail and deleting electronic spam.

CYBER STAT: Kaspersky Lab noted why spam is such a waste of time: "If spam reaches a user's inbox, a recipient has to delete it manually. A person who reads up to twenty e-mails per day may receive in the region of 180 spam messages along with their business correspondence. That means that they will spend five to six hours per month just deleting spam, to the detriment of their productive working time."
(Kaspersky Lab Securelist: *https://securelist.com/ threats/damage-caused-by-spam/1*)

QUICK TIP: Do not click on the bottom of a spam e-mail and ask to be removed from the "Do Not E-mail" list. You will likely receive more spam because they now know you are a real person and will then sell your name for more money to other spammers.

CHAPTER 10

GONE PHISHING AND SPOOFING

PHISHING IS SCAMS THAT USE FRADULENT E-MAILS and websites masquerading as legitimate businesses to lure unsuspecting users into revealing private account or login information. Pop-up messages often trick unsuspecting users into disclosing confidential information, as some users have trouble discerning if the pop-up is legitimate or from a cyberhacker. Other users will type anything the pop-ups ask, just so long as it stops nagging them.

Spoofing is accomplished when the spoofer creates a false copy of an actual website or e-mail in a way that misleads the recipient. Spoofing and phishing attacks are two peas in a pod. If phishing involves a net or phishing pole, then spoofing is the bait on the hook. The important part is that all of the network traffic between the target victim's browser and the fake or shadow page is sent through the spoofer's machine. This allows the spoofer to acquire personal information, such as passwords, credit card numbers, and account numbers. Even though the e-mail looks like the real thing, complete with authentic logos and working web links, it's actually a complete fake.

Keep in mind that if you are ever redirected to a website and asked to enter your account information, it is usually a scam. In some instances, talented phishers and spoofers direct you to the genuine website and then a window pops up over the site that captures your personal information. Of course the information the victim enters does not go to the legitimate site; it goes directly to the spoofer's account. And once they have captured it, it's too late. The cyberthief's ultimate goal is to take the information you entered and sell it directly to criminals who'll use it to ruin your credit and even attempt direct withdrawals of funds from your accounts.

iTunes Support Team !
To: info@bvsystems.com
Your AppleID Has been locked !

January 1, 2016 at 3:59 AM
Inbox - INFO

Hello Dear Customer,

• We had Some Problems With Your Account. Has Account Been Hacked,!! Please Update information The Account. if You Do Not Update information ,Your Account Will Be Closed !!

• To Update Your Account, You Can Confirm Your information, it's Easy.

Click here to validate your account

• Click the link below to open a window secure browser.
• Confirm that you are the account holder, then follow the instructions.
Thanks,
Apple Security Team.

I received this e-mail as part of a massive phishing attack against Apple users. The link takes you to another page that looks remarkably similar to an Apple login page. This bogus e-mail was sent to millions of users.

I always recommend you type the website directly into your browser if you want to visit any part of that site. If you see a phone number listed anywhere, call to see if an incentive is real or just to see if anyone actually answers. This is the minimum you can do to stay safe, and yet many phishing and spoofing scams do not go the extra mile to fool users with live receptionists or even believable voicemail messages. Internet scams are all about quantity and not quality. The scammers don't want to spend a little more time catching a big fish; they work by casting the biggest net over the most fish every time. The ones who get entangled were the lowest-hanging fruit; they were too slow, too naïve, or too confused to get out in time.

There is another telltale sign that you might not be

connecting to the URL you think you are. HTTP, or hyper-text transfer protocol, is a prefix appearing before every public website—whether you see it or not. HTTPS is the secured version of this protocol. (The "S" stands for "secure.") HTTPS is used to secure sensitive areas of websites, such as paywalls, logins, and other private areas of public websites. If you do not see the "S" in HTTPS and a website is asking for secure or private information, DO NOT PROCEED any further. Whether it's a spoof of a real website or an actual, legitimate website that just neglected to secure its payment area properly, you are at risk if you enter any private data about yourself. Remember the following:

If the URL does NOT include HTTPS in front of it, you have entered into an unsecured area.

If the URL DOES include HTTPS in front of it, you have entered into a secure area.

Many browsers also include a small lock icon to indi-cate that you have entered a secure HTTPS website.

You might wonder if people actually click on these attachments embedded in e-mails. Yes, every day many do, especially older individuals who might be more naïve. When an offer appears too good to be true, it is most likely a scam. An e-mail phishing attack can also often appear completely legitimate, so users will click on the link without a second thought. Cyberhackers use language and graphics in the body of the e-mail that look and feel like something you are comfortable with. These e-mails look no different than a dozen other e-mails from the same sender. We often feel a level of comfort with e-mails we have seen on a regular basis.

———————

QUICK TIP: Phishing attacks are one of the most popular and effective ways to lure you to click on an attachment in an e-mail you receive. Fight the urge, and DON'T click.

Phishing Attacks Statistics from: *www.getcybersafe.gc.ca*

Who takes the bait?

- 156 million phishing e-mails are sent every day by cyber criminals globally.
- Sixteen million e-mails make it through the SPAM filters.
- Eight million people open the e-mails.
- 80,000 people (or ten percent) fall for a scam every day and share their personal information.

CHAPTER 11

STRONG PASSWORDS TRUMP LAZY HACKERS

PASSWORDS ARE ESSENTIAL TO KEEP YOUR PRIVATE information private. If you ask the average person how many passwords they have they will probably say, "Too many!" I cannot disagree when I recall all the different passwords that I must remember: several bank accounts, stock trading, Facebook, LinkedIn, Twitter, Gmail, etc. The list goes on and on, and that is just my personal passwords. For business, I have well over fifty unique passwords tied to valuable online vendors and services. With cyberhackers eager to learn, use, and sell our passwords, we need to make their job as difficult as possible so that they simply move onto easier targets or give up altogether.

Unfortunately, the best way to manage your passwords is in direct conflict with the best way to keep your passwords secure. The passwords that are easiest to remember are also easiest for a stranger to crack, but there's no value in an insecure password so we must choose passwords that are difficult to crack. Do *not* use passwords based on personal information, such as a child or pet's name, your birthday, or the school you attended. In today's online world of social media, this information may not be as private as you would think. Many social users share this info freely and social websites make it all too easy. For instance, once someone "friends" you on Facebook, it will automatically remind you about that friend's birthday. When you consider how many people use all or part of their birth date in their usernames or passwords, it's like a password delivery service for lazy hackers.

CYBER STAT: "In 2014, forensic investigations have revealed that eighty percent of security breaches involve stolen and weak passwords." (CBS, "60 Minutes Explains Credit Card Hacking")

Choose a password that is at least fifteen alpha-numeric characters long and has a mix of numbers and symbols with uppercase and lowercase letters. A good example of a secure government payment site is the "Wide Area Work Flow" (WAWF), which the federal government uses as a secure website portal to submit invoices for electronic payment. That site requires a minimum fifteen-character password comprised of uppercase/lowercase/numbers/symbols. It requires the password to be changed every thirty days and prevents you from reusing a previous password.

A shocking statistic I came across was from Symantec: thirty-eight percent of Internet users would rather clean a toilet than make a new password! But secure passwords don't have to be difficult to create and remember. Acronyms of phrases or sentences make excellent pass-words that stay with you. The Quick Brown Fox Jumped Over The Lazy Dog is a mouthful but it's much easier to type TQBFJOTLD. Try picking a phrase that means something special to you and *only* you.

Change your passwords often; once a month is recommended for any sites containing banking, 401(k), or stock information. Create a regular schedule so that every time you wash your car (I wash mine once a month), you also change your financial passwords on that day, too. Whether it's every month or every six months, get into the habit. Millions of passwords are being bought and sold every day on the dark web. It won't take long for that simple password you created five months ago to be scraped and sold on a list of 100,000 other simple passwords. From there, it's only a matter of seconds before a hacker's software can match the right password used in conjunction with the right username or e-mail (also scraped and sold in a giant list). Once they login to your account, the damage can be instant or play out over an extended period of time. It all depends on their timetable and preferred approach.

Never use the same password across multiple sites, which is commonly known as "password reuse." It is certainly easy to remember one password, but if cyberthieves compromise that password, they will systematically use your stolen password to attempt to log into the most popular websites. This is akin to giving someone a master key to all the rooms in your house. They have only one key, but once they are in, they are free to roam about all of your rooms, looking through your drawers, closets, and even your safe.

Think you'll have trouble remembering all these new passwords? Download a password-management utility that stores your passwords in an encrypted file. There are password managers for every platform of PC, tablet, and smartphone. LastPass, Password Genie, and 1Password are well known and effective. They range in price from $10 to $30 to purchase the application, while some are subscription based. Of course, you need to create a single strong master password, which gets encrypted to use any of those apps, so everything discussed thus far still applies.

I have always felt the concept of LastPass, as well as other password managers, makes sense for users who would otherwise create simple, easy-to-remember, but hackable passwords, as opposed to long, strong, complex passwords with a password manager. Surely, having numerous passwords encrypted in the cloud is better than jotting them down on a sticky note that resides under your keyboard, right? The reason I personally do not use password managers is the distant fear of a major hack. What if my password manager gets hacked, and a hacker gets my master password? This would be tantamount to giving a thief the keys to my front door when I am heading off to vacation.

It seems my fears, as well as many other security experts' fears, have come to fruition with the announcement that LastPass was a victim of a targeted attack, and user information was compromised. On Monday, June 15, 2015, LastPass announced through a blog post that hackers had breached its databases and compromised e-mail addresses and password reminders, as well as encrypted master passwords. Apparently, they discovered the breach after detecting rather suspicious activity on their network.

Unfortunately, there is a percentage of LastPass users who will undoubtedly be the victim of targeted e-mail phishing attacks as a result of this breach. Phishing is an effective, focused attack where the cyber thugs send victims e-mails with an embedded link that fools users into revealing more data. LastPass users have been informed about this breach and the company recommend users update their LastPass master password. Cyberthieves have already keyed in on this and are no doubt readying focused e-mail phishing attacks that might have a message such as: "Update your LastPass master password immediately."

An unsuspecting LastPass user may click on the attachment and be redirected to a site that looks awfully close to LastPass but is just there to collect more information from unsuspecting users. They would be prompted to enter their old master password and then asked to create a new complex, stronger, secure password. Now the cyberhackers have the person's master password without having to steal it or decrypt it. The unsuspecting users have hand delivered this information directly to the hackers' servers.

Even though they did not get all the encrypted individual passwords, the breach could also result in other compromises, such as unlocking a user's e-mail account where you need the e-mail address and password reminder, thereby allowing them to gain access to your e-mail and a trove of other valuable private information.

If the hackers are truly advanced, there is a chance, although unlikely, that they could hack the encryption to crack the master password. This is extremely difficult, but then again, who would have thought a security company that provides encrypted password protection would ever be hacked in the first place? To make matters worse, this is actually the second breach LastPass has faced.

I personally use a little black book that I have easy access to but can also store in a secure place. I generally need to refer to it for at least one password daily but do not like to have my passwords stored on the computer or the cloud (i.e., some remote server I do not know the whereabouts of or can verify just how secure it is). This approach might seem a bit archaic for a cybersecurity expert, but let me explain: Hackers (and thieves in general) will always choose the simplest path to make their theft. Hackers might appear to be evil geniuses living in their parents' basements, but, in reality, they are just savvy computer users looking to make an easy living. They write some of their own code, but most steal or borrow the work of other hackers to make their "jobs" even easier. My point is that the last thing any of us has to worry about is a hacker physically breaking into our office to steal our little black book of passwords. We do not live in movies like *War Games* or *Hackers*. No legitimate hacker would ever risk breaking-and-entering charges when they can simply steal, trade, or sell private data from the safety and anonymity of their home. If they don't hit the jackpot with you, they'll simply move on to someone else. And even though they might peruse your profile on your social network of choice to gain access to your personal information, it's all rather impersonal.

I prefer to disable any cookies in my browser in the event I accidentally end up on open Wi-Fi or an unencrypted HTTP session because I might fall victim to a "man-in-the-middle" (MITM) attack. These network-eavesdropping attacks could intercept cookies and impersonate me to ultimately steal passwords and perform future malicious attacks. So I always recommend that users carefully monitor the URLs they visit to make sure they are designated as an HTTPS ("S" stands for secure) protocol. This ensures that all communication between my computer and the server employing Transport Layer Security (HTTPS protocol) is secure.

Be sure the actual number of password login attempts you have configured are limited. Some sites allow you to set a maximum number of tries before your account is locked. Enable this feature if the site offers it. You might recall hearing something about the iCloud celebrity nude photos hacking scandal in late 2014. It was all over the news for weeks, and for good reason. Finally, tech bloggers, TV network anchors, and cybersecurity pundits like me got to mention "iCloud," "celebrity," "hack," and "nude" all in the same breath. As you would expect, celebrity, tech, and mainstream news all picked up the story and ran with it for what felt like weeks.

I appeared on *Inside Edition* at the time to discuss the technical details of the breach into some celebrity iCloud users' accounts. As you could imagine, my ten-minute appearance via Skype was trimmed down to a tabloid-TV-friendly thirty seconds. After all was said and done, very few technical details were delivered to the public. Instead of learning from the celebrity security mistakes, we were treated to lectures on the evils and stupidity of taking naked selfies. And instead of practical security tips that normal users can apply, we were inundated with "iCloud Hacked" headlines. My point was that the iCloud network was actually not hacked, and this speaks directly to my suggestion for limiting login attempts. Due to security flaws in Apple's iCloud network, hackers were able to perform targeted attacks on *certain* users. A hacker used a software tool called iBrute to repeatedly try thousands of different password combinations to find information on those celebrities. Apple has since fixed this security flaw by limiting logins to only five password attempts, but there are still many popular sites that do not limit login attempts.

In mid-January 2015, I received a request to do a TV interview on a small business show called *Your Business* hosted by JJ Ramberg on MSNBC. I was to discuss cybersecurity and provide some practical tips small business owners would appreciate. One of the key elements JJ brought up was what constitutes a good password. I enjoy sharing tips, as there are many misconceptions about what a strong password is. Interestingly, at the end of the interview JJ asked if I had a second as she had a few more questions. She was blown away at how easy it was to hack a simple eight characters. JJ mentioned she was going to change her passwords immediately and, as I recommended, would not reuse the same password across multiple sites.

I feel it is important to not just tell people to create a strong password, but help them appreciate they are not alone. The vast majority of people choose simple passwords that are easy to remember and also easy to hack. I, too, was guilty of not creating strong passwords and reusing passwords that were easy to remember—that is, until I was hacked. There is still no reason to believe my hack was a result of a weak password I created, but how could I take the chance of future hacks by failing to observe one of the most basic tenets of cybersecurity? I encourage everyone who reads this to share with others the importance of creating strong passwords.

By now, you might have realized there are no foolproof solutions to password security. If hackers have the skills and want to get in, they will. Just like in the real world, security is about making your car or password as difficult to steal as possible, so a thief moves onto an easier target.

Remember, if you want to stay one step ahead of thieves, then think like them. They will always go for the easy password or the easy hack. When I ask myself to create a strong password, I think about the 1987 movie *SpaceBalls* when King Roland reveals the secret combination as 12345 and Dark Helmet says that is the stupidest combination and only an idiot would have it on his luggage. Mel Brooks then enters the scene asking for the secret combination and they reiterate "12345." Mel Brooks says, "That's the same combination on my luggage." Not much has changed in twenty-five years, as 12345 was still the second most popular password used in 2014.

Common numbers, words, and names are easy to remember but they are also easy to hack. In fact, any word appearing in the *Merriam-Webster Dictionary* can be hacked in less than one minute by an amateur hacker. This is because hackers always start with the lowest-hanging fruit. In this case, English speakers tend to use passwords derived primarily from an English dictionary. The entire English dictionary can be stored in RAM of any PC and then applied to tens of thousands of password attempts in seconds.

A good rule of thumb is that if any part of your password is closely associated to you, don't use it. The same holds true for part of your password, if any of the words can be found in the dictionary. If it is truly random and makes no sense to you, it will not be easily hacked. Here is an example of a reasonably strong password: TheBigCat3*8smells!

This password would take approximately sixty-two centuries to guess with a home computer, versus the one second it would take to guess the password 12345.

Many password hacks focus on software vulnerabilities. Brute force attacks are different in that they are a simple, targeted method of gaining access to a particular user's account. These attacks focus on passwords and user names by trying iterations of them over and over again until they get in. A brute-force attack is extremely effective when victims use easy, short passwords such as PASSWORD, admin, abc123, and everyone's favorite, 123456. Login information for many sites is usually a user's e-mail address, and we all know how easy it is for anyone to get that because we all receive spam. Couple this with a simple password and brute-force attacks suddenly allow hackers to compromise your login very quickly.

Enable two-factor authentication (also known as two-step verification) for sites and services you use to access your sensitive information, such as your banking, your cloud storage, your e-mail account, and online retailers that keep your credit or debit card on file. Two-factor authentication requires you to enter your password and another verification step, such as a PIN code texted to your cell phone. When the iCloud hack in 2014 hit, none of the compromised accounts had implemented two-factor authentication. In fact, *all* of the compromised accounts had weak passwords.

Quick Tip: Long, strong, and complex passwords are secure. Use an automatic password generator and a password strength indicator to verify how strong and secure a password truly is.

CHAPTER 12

GARDEN-VARIETY HACKERS

PENETRATION TESTERS SIMULATE CYBERATTACKS TO find security weaknesses and vulnerabilities in networks, operating systems, and applications. A penetration test is extremely useful because it helps to determine whether or not a computer system is vulnerable to an attack, before the actual attack. The current defense systems in place are stressed to see if they hold up or were defeated.

A simple illustration that comes to mind is the garden in the back corner of my yard a number of years ago. It was a perfect spot that I carefully cultivated, fertilized, and rototilled, so the soil was ideal. I planted tomatoes, peppers, string beans, watermelon, and lettuce. I quickly learned that growing a beautiful garden is rewarding, but it also attracts attention. One morning, I went outside to look at my garden and was alarmed to find a fat groundhog eating my vegetables. I quickly scared him off and decided it was time to put up my own defenses. I purchased some poles and a two-foot-high wire fence. It took some time and effort and, after all my work, I put up what I believed to be an impenetrable fortress. But to my surprise, the next day my furry friend was back and munching away again. Again I scared him off, but I did some investigating and noticed this time he had dug a small hole under my supposedly impenetrable fence.

I decided to dig a one-foot-deep trench around the perimeter of the garden and purchased a larger fence that I buried about one foot below the surface, with the top two feet above ground. Success! I managed to keep those lousy groundhogs out so I could finally enjoy the fruits of my labor. That groundhog was no different than your garden-variety cyberthief. Both groundhogs and hackers will always look for the hole or weakest point before they attempt to break in. They also both come back many times to that same hole to exploit it.

While penetration testing can expose many weaknesses, most organizations are hesitant to explore these vulnerabilities to learn more. Private companies or organizations want everything except their good news to be hidden from sight. Public companies have shareholders to answer to, so the last thing they're thinking about is telling the world about any network security holes they are patching up.

The most essential benefit of a penetration test is that it can determine the feasibility of a specific set of attack vectors. These vectors must be able to be applied repeatedly and in combination with other vectors. By controlling all parameters, the network in question can recreate any past or potential future attacks effectively. Unfortunately, this only ensures that the network will be safe from the *anticipated* attacks. You can only predict what you know, and that is why it is vital for penetration tests to be performed by outside parties.

Penetration tests are always best performed by a third party that is not part of the organization. This allows them to expose weaknesses that might otherwise be overlooked or not even challenged. Have you ever proofread your own work? No matter how many times you look at it, "accomodate" looks like it's spelled correctly. Then someone comes along and instantly points out the missing "m" in accommodate. Testing for security flaws in your own network is no different. If you are trying to save a buck by using a member of your own IT staff, they might be too defensive, unwilling, or unable to see the security problems staring them right in the face. You need a professional with experience, one who is aggressively looking for weaknesses to alert you to obvious vulnerabilities, because those very same vulnerabilities will be just as obvious to your attackers. You always want to see how your existing defenses handle actual hack attacks—or at least simulations of the real thing—before reinforcing, fortifying, or even rebuilding your network security.

Objective penetration tests might justify increased capital expenditures that will directly combat threats uncovered or holes that might be discovered. Typically, a basic vulnerability assessment runs around $3,000. A good vulnerability assessment will identify everything your network may be susceptible to. This is often followed by a more comprehensive penetration test, in which a small company might spend anywhere from $10,000 to $30,000, depending on the size of the organization and network. It typically takes anywhere from two to four weeks to complete a thorough penetration test. These tests are priceless because they reveal weaknesses in hardware, software, and infrastructure that a company's IT staff might overlook. Most often, they reveal the human element: people innocently divulging information, such as user names or passwords, without realizing they compromised the company's security.

———————

QUICK TIP: Companies should invest in independent vulnerability and penetration assessments. Do not try to save money by using your own IT department.

CHAPTER 13

WHAT COLOR HATS CAN HACKERS WEAR?

A HAT CAN PROTECT YOU FROM THE ELEMENTS, show off your style, or easily identify your profession. Hats vary in size, shape, and color, and can also be used to symbolize a particular social status. Hats worn in old Western movies stereotypically identified the villains as wearing black hats, while the good guys wore white hats. In a similar fashion, computer hackers can don many different hats, as well.

A "white hat" hacker intentionally breaks security to test a company's security system. A white hat is considered an ethical hacker who is *not* trying to maliciously hack a company's computer network. A white hat is trying to learn about the system's security vulnerabilities in the best way possible. These ethical hackers are individuals who are experts in understanding computer systems and exposing vulnerabilities for penetration tests and security assessments. Ultimately, a white hat is just pretending to be a black hat—only without the theft and malicious damage that usually follows the hack.

"Black hat" hackers are malicious and hack for personal or monetary gain. They sometimes form illegal hacking groups with fellow computer criminals. Black hats break into secure networks to destroy data or make the network unusable for authorized administrators and users. Some security-industry professionals also refer to black hats as "crackers." Crackers discover and keep the vulnerabilities private, so they can be exploited again in the future by themselves or by others willing to pay for the information. The hackers who targeted my company are likely black hats and have made it personal. The Lizard Squad is a prime example of a black hat hacker you should never mess with.

A "grey hat" hacker is one part white hat and one part black hat: Grey hats explore the Internet and hack into a computer system for the sole purpose of notifying the administrator they found a security hole in their system. Unlike other hackers, a grey hat will offer to correct the weakness free of charge. If white hats are like cops, and black hats are like criminals, then the grey hats are more like vigilantes. They operate illegally but do seem to follow a moral code of their own.

And the hats don't stop at just grey scale. A "red hat" is an aggressive hacker employed by a government agency, whose sole purpose is to hack into the computer networks of other governments. They are often trying to hurt or disable the other government, usually to further a political agenda or ideal they share or are being paid to spread. Stuxnet is believed to have been the cause of destruction of twenty percent of Iran's uranium enrichment infrastructure and was likely pulled off by red hats.

"Blue hats" are hired guns who hack because they are being paid by a company to do so. But they are hacking their own clients in order to discover and help repair security exploits. Over the years, Microsoft has hired many blue hats to find vulnerabilities in their Windows operating systems.

"Green hats" are new to the game. These novice hackers are also sometimes called "Script Kiddies." They are anxious to learn but also impetuous and naïve to the operations of their seasoned hacker brethren. Green hats are often the victims of their own curiosity. Like a child with an advanced chemistry set, Green hats can easily find themselves locked out or bricked by running a script they didn't write, much less understand.

QUICK TIP: Look in the mirror and make sure the hat you're wearing is the right color or you might end up behind bars.

CHAPTER 14

THE INSIDER THREAT

WITHIN ANY ORGANIZATION, even those most secretive to outsiders, open communication is essential. Everyone is connected through devices, and ultimately the Internet, so data must flow freely to and from the proper channels. No one expects unlimited transparency, so I like to pose a few questions to business owners about their employees who have access to confidential and proprietary information: Does the employee understand the importance of confidentiality, and does he/she keep the organization's information guarded and safe? We have all heard the expression: everyone has a price. Now imagine employees who feel they should have received more compensation or were overlooked for a promotion. Would they seek revenge? Would they leak a few passwords for a fast buck?

Dishonest employees can do more damage than external hackers or would-be cyberthieves. They have access to things like passwords, banking information, credit card information, social security numbers, and dates of birth—possibly both within the organization and its customer database. Such accessibility certainly might range from a database in the human resources department to setting up employee e-mails in the IT department. Whatever the case, employees often hold the keys to a treasure trove of data—a hacker's dream. We all want to believe everyone is above board and has the company's best interests in mind, but the second we let our guard down we might put our company, our career, and everyone else's at risk. If we view this as a looming possibility all the time, the chance of having an insider compromise the organization is largely diminished.

In an effort to tighten up internal security, it's sometimes easy to overlook the obvious. I always warn people not to put passwords on sticky notes on a monitor, under a keyboard, or in a desk drawer. Now as you are reading this, many of you are probably feeling guilty already because you are doing this, and that's understandable. Some positions require multiple passwords for multiple levels of security, and they must be accessed many times a day. The strongest passwords are the really complex ones with wacky characters that are much harder to remember, so we use little cheat sheets. It's difficult to remember the answers to some of those stupid security challenge questions because our favorite movies do change over time and older memories eventually fade.

It sounds a bit paranoid, but a computer plastered with sticky notes full of passwords is a billboard advertising security leaks. And when you get up for a coffee or bathroom break, it only takes a few seconds for someone to walk by your desk and snap a photo with their smartphone. From there, that little one-sixtieth of a second exposure is sold to the highest bidder, who then puts it through its Photoshop paces to zoom and enhance on every single digit. You would be amazed at the amount of visual information a decent smartphone pic can capture in less than a second. String a few more incidents like these together within the same company and you have the makings for a company-wide hack. Massive security audits, layoffs, and ransomware payouts are soon to follow.

You are far better off to have a little black book with all your user names, challenge questions, and passwords that you access daily. Keep your black book secured in a fireproof safe or under lock and key, preferably in a secured office. The ritual of unlocking and pulling out a black book to remember complex passwords will keep your data safe and force you to do what you should have already been doing: learn those most commonly used passwords by heart. Or come up with your own little system. So long as there is at least one physical component that is out of sight and secure from others, you have your key for your lock. We'll always have some kind of physical lock on our front doors or computers but each factor alone is worthless without the other, so one must be kept hidden and nearby for both our own convenience and security. Make sure your computer has a user name and password requirement upon startup and screen saver mode so no one has access to anything when you are away from your computer. Use caution if you must have remote access to your computer or share files on the network. I like to completely shut down my computer each evening and start up fresh in the morning with my secure login. It's not only safer but also minimizes the number of annoying freezes or crashes on most Mac and Windows PCs. If someone physically breaks in, they might just grab the computer and spend the time later pulling off confidential or proprietary information. This is certainly more challenging if your machine requires a secure login upon start up. Set up your tablet or smartphone to require a complex unlocking PIN or biometric fingerprint detection in the event it is lost or stolen. Four PIN digits are never enough. A good thief doesn't even need to know your PIN in order to gain access to your phone within seconds. There are several advanced chemical, thermal, and optical techniques that allow thieves to determine a four-digit PIN sequence without seeing a single digit.

QUICK TIP: It only takes one corrupt employee within an organization to commit a successful cyber crime. Report all suspicious activity to your employer, as you never know when you have an insider threat.

CHAPTER 15

THE WIRELESS THREAT

THIEVES LOOK FOR VULNERABILITIES when breaking into a facility, such as an unlocked door or window, or even a computer that is not password protected. They might evade security cameras or personnel, but all of these physical security measures can be challenging to overcome as a thief might be noticed and caught. Suspicion is easily raised at any stage when trying to physically break in and compromise security.

With wireless technology becoming ever more cost effective and easier to implement, many cyberthieves look to wireless as the conduit to hack their way inside a network. Back in the late 1980s, Berkeley Varitronics Systems (BVS) was approached by a Washington, DC, firm, Lunayach Communications Consultants (LCC), to help resolve a wireless design issue they faced. They needed to simulate wireless coverage before expensive build outs, and that could only be accomplished with test equipment and advanced software that allowed them to plot out detailed maps they could sell to carriers. LCC contracted BVS to design advanced cellular test equipment that LCC sold to carriers such as Cellular One, Nextel, and Sprint. We were thrilled to be chosen as their supplier for both design and manufacturing of this advanced test equipment.

I oversaw the production team and Gary Schober, BVS CTO, turned the LCC account over to me to focus on the business side while he focused on the wireless-design side. Gary has the uncanny ability to look at a complex problem and come up with a cost-effective and innovative solution. His head for business built BVS from scratch over forty years ago, but his engineering side makes him a truly exceptional CTO.

Meanwhile, the wireless carriers had a daunting task. Not knowing how many cell towers they needed or where best to place them, installers and technicians were often left to guess. This was compounded by the fact that an average cell tower would take approximately one year from start to finish to erect and light up. It was imperative for carriers to properly engineer the wireless networks to maximize the number of wireless callers each tower could handle and monetize a return on their investment that much quicker. Since the build out of these networks could take decades, tower placement became key.

BVS still designs and builds cellular propagation test equipment for wireless carriers around the world. Much of the expertise and understanding of how these advanced wireless networks behaved also taught us how they operate, as well as the vulnerabilities that cyberthieves could exploit. By having a firsthand understanding, our engineers were able to respond and develop advanced security tools that are now effectively used to combat wireless threats.

When talking to different organizations and individuals about their networks, I realize all too often that wireless threats go unrealized and overlooked. This is usually because IT administrators are competent at setting up and securing their wired networks but not very familiar with the wireless component. In 2000, the Institute of Electrical and Electronics Engineers (IEEE) ratified a new emerging wireless standard that was to be used in the license-free 2.4 GHz spectrum; it came to be known as the ubiquitous Wi-Fi we all use today. The FCC made sure there was spectrum available to companies outside that frequency so wireless cell phones could operate without interference, but microwave ovens, cordless phones, and wireless baby monitors all inhabited that 2.4 GHz space; therefore, a solution was needed.

BVS developed a Wi-Fi analysis tool called the Grasshopper, which tested the signal strength of various Wi-Fi 802.11b networks. Grasshopper became an overnight success, and we added several unique and advanced features, including spectrum analysis, which allows engineers to visualize RF energy in the form of unlicensed 2.4 GHz interference.

Companies like Apple Computer quickly saw the value of Wi-Fi for their planned move into a truly mobile space. They learned about our Grasshopper and became one of our first customers by inviting us to exhibit at their annual trade show at the Jacob Javitz Center in NYC known as MacWorld. I will never forget the first show we exhibited at, where we were attacked by interested parties flocking to our booth to see the only known tool used to install access points and measure signal strength, channel number, and Service Set Identification (SSID) network identifiers, which is the name assigned to a wireless network. Within the year, we were selling hundreds of Grasshoppers to any company looking to install wireless networks. Universities followed suit as prices of Wi-Fi access points began to drop. Soon, mainstream consumer adoption took hold in the form of low cost routers, cards, and ad-hoc networks.

The Wi-Fi explosion has transformed the way we connect to each other and the Internet of Things (IoT). Mobile phones, tablets, and computers are now all connected effortlessly to each other and the Internet. But with all the breakthrough technology innovations, there is also a dark side. Cyberthieves lurk about to find the next vulnerability, and Wi-Fi is just another conduit for such behavior.

Wi-Fi was designed to allow short-range wireless access from a device, such as a laptop, to your local network. Sometimes we take for granted how dependent we are on Wi-Fi. During a recent New Jersey winter blizzard, our cable modem went down. After several hours of downtime, I was feeling a bit restless as I am on the computer a good ten-plus hours a day, handling e-mails, business proposals, quotations, social media, banking, stock market, writing . . . you get the point. So when the Wi-Fi is down, I find myself thinking more about what I cannot do, rather than working. Just as I was about to relent and get off the computer for the day, I remembered that I had purchased a 4G Verizon LTE hotspot for when I travel and need Internet access. I decided to set this up in my house so I could stay connected, and it worked great.

My motivation for getting the LTE hotspot came purely as a result of my frugality. Every trade show we have ever exhibited at would charge exorbitant fees for basic Wi-Fi Internet access. A few years ago, BVS was exhibiting in Barcelona at the GSM World Congress show, one the biggest wireless shows in the world. Since the show spans five days, I wanted to get some work done between customer visits to our booth. I figured they would charge a pretty penny as they had a cap-tive audience, but to my amazement, they wanted over $1,000 for a Wi-Fi connection.

There are levels of security implemented within the Wi-Fi protocol, yet many customers who purchase an access point set it up and leave it set to the unse-cure factory default. In my unscientific research I have discovered that every neighborhood I visit contains a few open, unsecured access points. An open access point is analogous to leaving the front door wide open for a thief to come in and rob you. A cyberthief can simply pull into your neighborhood or perhaps into the industrial park where they are targeting your corporation and with a laptop, directional antenna, some hacking software, and an overpriced cup of Starbucks coffee, they can access your private network before their coffee even gets cold.

They typically start by scanning for an open access point. Of course they can also identify your network quickly by your SSID. Once they have your access point identified and are connected to it, they get busy hacking further past your firewall and directly into your computer files.

Also, before you identify your network by assigning an SSID, keep in mind this is broadcast to anyone within a quarter mile, and thus they know who and where you are. For example, if your SSID is "Smith Home," a quick Internet search on Google with your street and home number may confirm yes the Smith home is the target, and they start to infiltrate your wireless network. The same is true in the corporate world; if your business is a target, you would not want your SSID to have your business name. Find a unique name that would not associate that SSID to your locality.

This being said, the vast majority of SSIDs are home-owners' names, or business names one would make an instant connection with. This is often because when a homeowner or business owner is setting up their wire-less access point, they are not thinking about security, but rather excited to set up their network and get started. After BVS was hacked, we immediately changed our SSID and our password for our company's wireless network so there was no association to our business for a potential hacker.

With the proliferation of the cell phones to where just about everyone on the planet can now afford one, security becomes a serious issue. Currently more cell phone accounts are activated than there are people on the face of the earth. Modern smartphones have integrated Wi-Fi, Bluetooth, cellular, and NFC (near field communication) as standard, built-in configurations. These various means of communication make cell phones ideal for communications across many platforms, but they also make them easy targets for hackers to exploit.

Several government agencies have requested BVS to offer lower-cost tools to detect and locate any wireless threats that might endanger a secure facility that houses confidential information. These secure facilities prohibit wireless devices, and that can be extremely challenging to enforce because many wireless devices are becoming smaller and smaller, while at the same time are increasing features. Imagine this scenario: A discreet thief (perhaps a cleared government contractor) could enter a sensitive compartmented information facility (SCIF) where US military classified information is housed, snap a few photos of classified material with a smartphone, and immediately e-mail pictures to a third party on the outside in a matter of minutes. When the compromised photos are transmitted to the third party, they could easily cover their tracks by immediately erasing the evidence on their phone. Sounds too simple, but this is reality with wireless technology. It can be anywhere at any time, and that includes the wrong place at the wrong time.

BVS also has the PocketHound in our security arsenal. The PocketHound is an effective security tool to detect and locate unauthorized cell phones in SCIFs and wireless-free security zones within any facility. Many schools and universities quickly learned that the product was ideal for catching cheating students looking up answers on their mobile phones during exams. News spread as teachers and their universities around the globe began ordering and recommending PocketHound.

Jon Leiberman and I discuss security issues and cheating students on his Sirius XM show.

But what got the ball rolling and the word out about PocketHound was my interview back in mid-2013 with Jon Leiberman on his Sirius XM Radio show. We talked about various security concerns and tools that address those issues. The conversation then shifted toward education and, specifically, how PocketHound can help educators catch cheating students. You will recall Jon's foray into national investigative reporting on the long-running TV show *America's Most Wanted*. His perspective is a great sounding board for security matters, both traditional and wireless threats affecting all our lives.

———————————

QUICK TIP: The wireless threat is often the most attractive means a cyberthief will exploit first to gain access to a computer network. Make sure to use an obscure SSID and long, strong passwords when you set up your wireless network.

CHAPTER 16

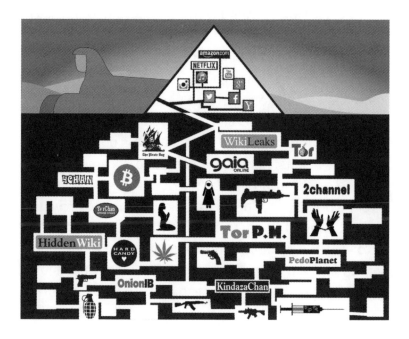

THE DARK WEB

THE WORLD WIDE WEB IS A VAST AND EVER-CHANGING network of web pages. In the early days of the web, there were no search engines, and people relied on finding information using pages with long lists of HTML links. It was cumbersome and links were often outdated. The development of automated search engines made it much easier for users to find information. Modern search engines like Google, Yahoo, and Bing use programs called "spiders" that crawl (meaning search) the web for links between the main page on a site and its subpages that meet the search criteria. These publicly viewable pages are part of what is called the "surface web," but they're just the tip of the Internet iceberg.

You might wonder what's just below the surface web. While the web is growing constantly, cybersecurity experts know the vast majority of web pages are inaccessible to search engines. For example, subpages on public web servers that are not linked to other pages do not show up in search results; however, if someone knows the page's URL, he or she can directly access the page by typing it into the browser's address bar. Hidden pages can include unpublished blog posts, forums that force users to log in to view the contents, and news sites that archive their stories for paid subscribers only after a specific amount of time. Collectively, these resources that are, in effect, hidden from search engines are called the "deep web," also known as the "dark web." The information locked away in the deep web is valuable. Doctors could access information currently hidden in archived databases about new research and medical procedures. Aerospace engineers could find data on how to build safer airplanes. Unfortunately, cybercriminals also use the dark web for communication and to hide their illicit activities. The deep web also contains pages where criminals use a type of digital currency called Bitcoin to trade and sell everything from stolen credit card numbers to illegal drugs—a virtual black market.

Navigating this deep web is a little different than the surface web, since it is not indexed by the normal search engines we are accustom to using. It requires browser software called "the onion router," or Tor for short, because these deep-web sites are called "onion sites." See *http://en.wikipedia.org/wiki/Tor_(anonymity_network)*. Tor is a network of donated servers run by volunteers around the globe, and it also anonymizes users by bouncing their web traffic through a randomized series of encrypted servers located around the world. This makes Tor users much more difficult to track online, which is exactly what the nefarious users want.

For example, say you are located in Maryland and want to access a web page on a server in Australia. Under normal circumstances, you would type in the URL and the data (also known as "packets") take a more or less direct route from your computer to the Australian server and back. With Tor, the data packets may bounce through extensive network relays (servers) anywhere in the world, and at each step the traffic is encrypted. Each relay only knows where the packet came from and where it is going next. No single computer in the chain knows the entire route. This is what makes Tor users so difficult to identify. (Note: Onion sites ending with .onion are hosted as Tor hidden services and are layered and encrypted for secure anonymity.)

Like the deep web itself, Tor does have legitimate uses. The software was developed by the United States government to protect whistleblowers, dissidents who live under repressive political regimes, and others who would be in danger if their identities were compromised. Some governments (like China, for example) censor the surface web, blocking certain websites and monitoring their citizens' online activities. Facebook recently established a direct connection to Tor, allowing users in these areas anonymous access to its site. Tor also protects those who simply value their privacy and aren't doing anything illegal but don't want their browsing habits tracked. To be fair, Tor has been embraced by lawful users, but it also provides ways for cybercriminals, terrorists, and other bad guys to avoid identification. This has made breaking Tor's anonymity a top priority for government agencies, both at home and abroad.

The United States government seems to be of two minds about Tor. On one hand, Tor is a brainchild of the US military. Initially, Tor was designed by the US Naval Research group in the mid 1990s, and "onion routing" was further developed by Defense Advanced Research Projects Agency (DARPA) in 1997. Onion routing is a technique for anonymous communication over a computer network, in which messages are put in layers of encryption, similar to the layers of an onion. It was created to protect whistleblowers and journalists operating in restricted areas from repartitions. In 2012, over half of the Tor Project's revenue came from government grants.

On the other hand, the National Security Agency (NSA) has been working to unmask Tor users, but they have been less successful in separating one Tor user from another. Many governments cannot use the NSA's technique for separating Tor traffic from normal traffic because they lack the close ties to telecom companies or the ability to monitor large swaths of Internet activity in real time.

It is interesting to note that Russia's Ministry of the Interior ran a contest for Russian nationals and companies with a goal of finding a workable method of deanonymizing Tor users. The grand prize? A contract worth four million rubles, equivalent to $111,000 USD. News reports indicated the contract was awarded, but the Russian government did not name the winner.

While the Chinese government has been silent on what efforts they are taking to unmask Tor users, it is known they have taken the approach of blocking access to the Tor software and public relays. The "Great Firewall of China" is capable of deep packet inspection and can identify and block nonpublic relays based on specific protocols unique to Tor. However, it is possible for Tor users in China to get around these blocks using different techniques.

The Tor Project has a small core number of employees, but uses a network of volunteers and crowdsourced labor to patch vulnerabilities and keep its users anonymous. When the annual Black Hat Security Conference announced a panel on how to deanonymize Tor users, the team went to work on closing the loophole before the conference even took place. It seems that for now, though, Tor will remain a useful tool for those who wish to keep their online activities secret.

I often wonder when our checking account and credit card was compromised. Did cyber thieves post our stolen credentials in the underground dark web? How much did they sell this for, before a thief cashed in? What did they buy with our stolen funds? These questions continue to weigh on my mind as I continually warn others of the unnerving dark web and the cyberthieves who prowl there. I am confident that when the cyberhackers targeted my company, they were navigating in the dark web anonymously using Tor.

———————

CYBER STAT: The Parliamentary Office of Science & Technology in Great Britain deemed the Tor with nearly 2.5 million users to be "by far the most popular anonymous internet communication system."

PART 3

STAYING SAFE

CHAPTER 17

SECURITY PLAYBOOK

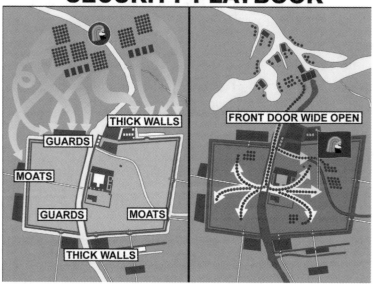

EFFECTIVE SECURITY ACHIEVED IN LAYERS

ONE THING THAT CONTINUES TO FASCINATE ME is just how much we can learn from history. My misfortunes in security and lax complacency in the past will hopefully aid others so they do not fall prey to cyberhackers. We can all learn from our mistakes and those of others that properly applying basic precautions can prevent you from becoming the next victim. One of the first monumental security breaches actually happened a long time ago, back in 732

BC, when the prophet Isaiah put in writing a prophecy concerning the demise of mighty Babylon some 200 years in advance. This prophecy came true in 539 BC, when Babylon was overthrown by Medo-Persian armies, resulting in the city becoming a heap of ruins, as was predicted.

What happened? Before it was overthrown, Babylon was a fertile plain situated some fifty miles south of what is now modern Baghdad. This land was described as a magnificent city filled with majestic temples, towers, and lush gardens throughout. Many referred to Babylon as the "City of Wonders," and to this day it is considered one of the greatest cities of the ancient world. From a security perspective, the city of Babylon seemed impregnable. The inner wall was over twenty-one feet thick, and the outer wall (situated some twenty feet away) was over eleven feet thick. Babylon rested on the banks of the Euphrates River with moats that surrounded the city's massive double walls. Two centuries earlier, both Isaiah and Jeremiah prophesized that Babylon's rivers or canals fed by the Euphrates River would dry up.

The Babylonians were so confident and secure behind their walls and with the city's defenses that on the night of the attack, many were involved in a large feast. Babylonian King Belshazzar was feasting with a thousand of his subjects, feeling safe and secure behind his massive defenses. The prophet Daniel interpreted a riddle that had mysteriously appeared on a wall for King Belshazzar: his kingdom was finished and would soon be given over to the Medes and the Persians. It was literally "handwriting on the wall," and to this day the saying "the handwriting on the wall" means a clear failure or catastrophe is imminent. That seemingly impregnable city was to soon face a challenge against its security defenses. True to the recorded prophecy, Cyrus the Great, who was upstream from Babylon, had his men divert the Euphrates, causing the water level in the city to fall. This afforded the soldiers the opportunity to wade through the river toward the city gates, which were left open. This catastrophic blunder led to Babylon's demise. (Source: *www.jw.org.*)

Here lies a good lesson from history. Layers of security are essential, but your security defenses are only as strong as your weakest layer. So much emphasis had been placed on Babylon's immense walls that little thought was given to the river flowing right into the city as their water source. They even ignored the prophecies that clearly spoke of the river drying up, but the warnings could not overcome Babylon's hubris.

When companies think about cybersecurity and the necessary layers required to properly protect their networks, they need to focus on the weakest layer because this is surely the layer any cyberhackers will also focus upon. Perhaps a cyberhacker wants to plant malware on a company's server. They might try to exploit the company's Wi-Fi network by hacking the password to gain access. These same hackers might also look for a "backdoor" to get an e-mail through the company's firewall. A backdoor in a computer system is a method of bypassing normal authentication, securing unauthorized remote access to a computer. What about the unsuspecting employee who is handed a USB stick and plugs it directly into a computer on the company's network? This is clearly an insider threat. In all these instances, it is essential for corporations to put the best layers of security in place, while making sure they do not neglect the most obvious ones like the front door.

Firewalls are effective defenses for preventing unknown traffic from coming through and causing havoc to the computer network. If there are no defenses in place and suspicious traffic is allowed to come through the firewall, this could compromise the network's security. Some of the more modern firewalls have advanced analytics that provide IPS (Intrusion Prevention System) and traffic inspection, allowing the firewall to summarily delve into the packets and detect malicious traffic automatically. Therefore, a firewall will make a hacker's life more difficult. Unfortunately, hackers are aware of the extra effort they need to put forth to breach a firewall by making the connection look like standard HTTP traffic. The average firewall will allow harmless-looking HTTP traffic to pass through without inspection. No firewall is one hundred percent secure, but having a good firewall in place forces hackers to adjust their tactics and find the next-weakest layer or motivate them to move on to an easier target.

Modern firewalls can analyze the traffic looking for security anomalies. These anomalies are sometimes just harmless packets that happen to look suspicious. In either case, the user must step in to either allow or quarantine the packets, but at least the packets have been flagged. If you think about how data flows in and out of a monitored network, good analytics can observe that flow between the internal host and the one on the Internet. Flow collectors can analyze and collect the source and destination

IP addresses, as well as the ports. They can provide information, such as how much data (in bytes) were actually transmitted. All of this deeper analysis will provide a visual pattern of traffic and any anomalies will set off a red flag when they are out of the norm.

What is unusual activity? If high bandwidth traffic is observed, this is an anomaly that is flagged. Exceptionally long and really slow connections might also raise the red flag, as this might indicate data is being stolen over a prolonged period of time and the hacker is trying not to get noticed. In any case, large data transfers should be analyzed carefully.

Antivirus protection is another important layer. By itself, antivirus software provides minimal protection, but when implemented in the layered approach, antivirus becomes yet another vital security strategy. Antivirus software aids in protecting the network from malware, but it is only as good as its latest update. With so many new viruses and Trojan horses hitting the web daily, antivirus software must be updated frequently to stay ahead of—or at least up to speed with—past and present hacking efforts. This continues to be the weakest layer of security within the antivirus security layer itself, because it requires users to regularly update and launch antivirus software, no matter how annoying the pop-up warnings are that continue to nag users.

Cyberthieves are savvy at analyzing how the latest update in antivirus software works so they can find a means to circumvent the antivirus antidote almost immediately. The top hackers will run their malware against antivirus software before deploying an attack, to make sure they are not detected. After we were hacked, I have religiously updated to the latest security patches for our company's Operating System (OS). Perhaps I was too complacent in the past by relying on the regular OS updates, which contributed to the multiple hacks we endured.

Securing your endpoints (meaning the mobile devices often remote from your PC and firewall) can provide protection beyond antivirus software to centrally manage the specific PCs or devices that have access, and which particular applications they can use. When you hear of layered security, it means the goal is to slow down potential hackers. If you can effectively deploy layers of security, hopefully you will detect them and thwart the attack before your computer network is infiltrated. Keep in mind that a determined hacker will eventually penetrate even multiple layers of security.

Time is of the essence when malware is detected; ideally, an immediate alert to the user should be generated so the malware can be located and removed quickly from the network. Any exploited vulnerabilities must be fixed in a timely fashion before the security breach could possibly expand to other computers on the network. Let history be a lesson so we can benefit in making sure all our layers of security are up to par.

———————

QUICK TIP: Cyberhackers are lazy, and they will look for the path of least resistance to get into your computer's network. Keep in mind that hackers will always exploit the easy and most obvious weaknesses you may not even realize, such as leaving open the front door.

CHAPTER 18

SECURITY IS EVERYONE'S BUSINESS

REFLECTING BACK ON ALL THE BREACHES, credit card fraud, and hacks I've experienced, the one lesson I can never let myself forget is that I am not alone. When asked to present on the topic of security, I like to get the audience involved, and when I ask if anyone has ever experienced a breach or has been the victim of identity theft or credit card fraud, I always get the same reaction: First, it's hesitation; no one wants to admit it, so they look around the room to make sure they are not alone in divulging something that might imply they are lax on security. After a minute and a few more pointed security questions, eighty percent of the hands typically go up. I point out the twenty percent of the hands you do not see up have already had their information compromised, but just don't know it yet. That usually gets a chuckle, but it also makes my point. Security is now everyone's business, and it touches all our lives as consumers, employees, business owners, and even world leaders.

Security is now at the forefront of everything I do within my company and my personal life. I share as much information as I can with everyone I come in contact with so they can protect themselves as well. I continue to have incredible opportunities interacting with world leaders to find out how they deal with serious security issues. In 2011 I received an invitation as a VIP guest to the Concordia Summit, held in New York City ten years after the anniversary of the September 11 attacks, for a reason. Much of the dialogue surrounded the role security has played in our lives, particularly after 9/11.

BVS is often contacted by law enforcement when technical assistance and advice are needed. Immediately after the devastating attacks on the World Trade Center in NYC, we were approached by government agents about how to "direction find" the cell phones that victims trapped in rubble might still have on their person. At that time, this technique was done with spectrum analyzers and direction-finding antennas; it was rather cumbersome when compared to the tools we offer today. Our tips and recommendations were well received and allowed them to better focus their search-and-rescue efforts for possible victim locations by detecting sporadic phone activity.

The Concordia Summit was designed to bring business leaders and world leaders together to discuss security concerns and share ideas. There were approximately 150 attendees and a few dozen speakers, so it was truly an intimate VIP event that encouraged networking among rather uncommon allies, such as business and political leaders. While numerous press people attended the event, they were sequestered behind velvet ropes and ultimately confined to a pressroom.

As I approached the entrance, I noticed a dozen long, black stretch limousines lined up. These were not your traditional rented prom limos. They looked intimidating from the outside, made to withstand explosive blasts, and they were parked everywhere. Speakers at this event included Homeland Security Advisor Frances Townsend; Governor Tom Kean, Acting Chair to the 9/11 Commission; and President George W. Bush—and that was just the first glance. The international presence includes numerous present and former presidents, such as the presidents of Georgia, Colombia, and Poland. John Negroponte (who served during George W. Bush's presidency as the US ambassador to Iraq, and was the first Director of National Intelligence and the Deputy Secretary of State) was also presenting. As the event unfolded, I realized these political leaders were actually looking to business leaders like me for advice, so that set my mind at ease.

I grabbed a coffee and had something to eat as I tried to match the names from the program with the faces in my room. I did not recognize any of the speakers listed in the program from my room but one of the attendees introduced himself to me, and we exchanged business cards. He asked what my company did and I gave him a brief overview of our security tools. I asked about his line of work and he turned out to be a children's heart surgeon who was invited to find out how the latest advances in security would spill out from my sector and over into healthcare. A big concern was people bringing cell phones to unauthorized areas in his hospital.

The summit consisted of national leaders discussing the security challenges they face, followed by Q&A with various business leaders. During the over-the-top luncheon, I was tapped on the shoulder for an interview request. My last bite of caviar-smothered salmon would have to wait as I raced out for a quick interview. A professional media crew hired by Concordia to interview select VIP guests had already set up the lights, camera, and a backdrop. All they needed now was a talking head like me. A young reporter greeted me, said she had some questions, and wanted to jump right in. I actually prefer this kind of impromptu questioning, so long as we are both on the same page.

"Do you think the world leaders will ever solve the global security problems and the threat of further terrorist threats as a result of this event?" she unabashedly asked.

"Politicians will certainly try to counter the threats, but they will surely fail," I responded. She looked at me as if I had missed the question.

I reaffirmed and rephrased my response with, "I am

sure that some have good intentions, but they will not succeed."

As I spoke, she was nodding in agreement, but she was clearly looking for something more like, "This event will foster change and make the world a safer place, etc."

But I was not going to provide the rhetoric those before and after me would surely give. If she was fishing for a particular quote to use, she would have to get that from someone else. It's sometimes difficult or awkward to stay true to what you feel and believe, especially when a camera is in your face, but I am no one's mouthpiece. That is why I am happy to avoid the world of politics, as it is filled with people focused more on tickling the ears of the listeners and their constituents for the sake of their party or reelection. Fortunately, the world of business and security is more binary and results driven, so you can be yourself without worrying about another agenda.

As the summit came to a conclusion, I was happy to have glimpsed into the everyday lives of world leaders. I am truly grateful that my day job doesn't involve making tough security calls. Suffice it to say, I would make a bad politician.

CHAPTER 19

TNL EXCLUSIVE

HACKED AGAIN!
CTO ADMITS BIGGEST SECURITY
BREACH IN COMPANY'S HISTORY
OVER 20 MILLION USER ACCOUNTS AFFECTED

TECH
NEWS
LIVE

STOCK PLUMMETS ... MICROSOFT POSTPONES BUYOUT TALKS ...

TAKE CONTROL OF YOUR SECURITY

AS WE CONTINUE TO GROW Berkeley Varitronics Systems, I look forward to the next forty years where I can hopefully pass the reins onto my children to continue. My father always told me to learn from his mistakes and to know what not to do in business. I try my best to do this and, at the same time, reflect on the forty years of success stories we have had the privilege in bringing to life. In the world of security, no news is good news, so I feel a tremendous amount of satisfaction when a customer expresses appreciation for a product that has saved a life, a bank account, a network, or just made a difference. We don't generally get to hear the good stories. Those just happen every day, if we do our jobs right and our customers do their jobs right. Whether it is preventing the next wireless hack or preventing an accident with our distracted driving cell phone monitoring system, when someone asks for security advice and then feels safer, I feel great.

Gary Schober instilled a strong work ethic in me through the years as both my father and boss. This is not something anyone can learn in a textbook, but can only be fully understood when you live it. Working in one company through my entire life has helped me to be determined, to never accept complacency and to appreciate every employee has something to contribute. I have learned I personally will not excel at everything but I can surround myself with people that are gifted beyond my means, in order to build and maintain a strong team. My brother, Craig (our media director), has creative ability that I will never possess when it comes to video production or design and layout in the visual arts. As the President and CEO of a technology company, I'm acting as a conductor to keep the entire orchestra in sync, making adjustments as needed. I have learned that technology, when embraced properly, can make life more enjoyable. Misuse of technology, on the other hand, can distract and consume you, pulling everything you care for into a vortex that eats up your precious time.

Our core business model and principles are timeless, yet we continually are re-inventing our business through novel solutions in the world of wireless and cyber threats. A distinct advantage we have as a small wireless company is that we are always following the newest emerging wireless standards, often developing test tools before anyone else in order to deploy that latest technology first. Cyberhackers are on a similar path in that they, too, are always using technology and exploiting the latest vulnerabilities. I think this is one of the challenges I embrace most. Knowing that cyberhackers are always looking to exploit vulnerabilities and need to stay one step ahead of the latest security technology is what drives me. I have the understanding and ability to thwart their attacks and provide effective security tools and advice that keep people and their companies secured.

In October 2014, I received a call from an Associated Press (AP) business writer. They were doing a special feature on small businesses that were victims of cyber-crimes. I had just wrapped up an interview with Trish Regan from *Street Smart* on BloombergTV about the JP Morgan Chase breach. The business writer was developing the story and explained it was challenging to find business owners willing to go on record to discuss their own security failures. She also wanted to understand how the dynamics of how all the recent cyberbreaches affect business owners' motivation to increase their security investments.

At the onset of the conversation, I was a bit guarded and felt hesitant to share every detail in my answers. Should I share that my company had been hacked and had been a victim of credit card fraud? There was a natural sense of embarrassment, but pride shrivels up when you realize you never want anyone else to go through the same emotional roller coaster a cyberhack takes you on. We chatted for a good fifteen minutes as I shared my story, and I could hear the keyboard clicks synchronized to my responses. After doing over a hundred phone interviews in the past two years for reporters, editors, producers, and business writers, I can quickly anticipate where the conversation is headed, so it has become easier to speak extemporaneously. And in this case, I was not just sharing tips on how to stay safe, but rather speaking from the victim's perspective after my company's bank account was compromised.

When the breach first hit my company, I felt the entire emotional spectrum, from embarrassed to frustrated to angry and even vengeful. But in the midst of this interview and reliving some of my victimization, I knew it was important to maintain my composure. Interviewers tend to fixate on the more dramatic and sensational elements of the story, so you never fully know what they will print. I strived to stay the course and tell my story honestly, with just enough facts and details but not too much introspection. The interview ended well but with no certainty or promises of publication.

To my surprise, the next morning I received a phone call from an AP photographer asking if he could swing by my office to get a photo to go along with the story. The photographer came by the next day and was excited about the story. He asked a lot of product-related questions and also about our capabilities as a company. I always appreciate it when people want to learn more about what BVS offers, so I gave him the mini-grand tour of our Metuchen, New Jersey, headquarters. He thought a photo of me in a few different areas around our products would make for some great shots, a few in our labs, a few on the production floor, and a few up in the office. He stayed about an hour and took several thousand photos, literally. I inquired as to why so many photos were necessary, and he said he was looking for the perfect shot.

The next morning, I got on my computer as usual to scan the latest news and check out the latest cyber-breaches in the headlines. This sometimes will give me a heads up if it is going to be a quiet day or if there is a breaking story that gets my phone ringing. On more than one occasion, I have just finished reading a breaking story when my phone rings or my e-mail chimes and it's my publicist telling me I'm scheduled to appear on that very story in a just a few hours. Staying current with cyber-breaches is essential, as time is never on your side. On this day, a *USA Today* headline caught my eye because it read: "Hacking a Big Danger for Small Business."

Halfway through the article I realized that I was the subject, and my photograph taken the day before was included. I read the article twice in a row and was happy for BVS to get this exposure. I then Googled my name and saw hundreds of other publications had also picked up the article, including *The New York Times, The Washington Post,* and *Inc.* magazine. I even counted up to six different photos throughout various articles. I later learned that AP offers a service to various newspapers, magazines, and online media in which they sell stories and photos to publications looking for the latest news trends. I supposed it's a mixed blessing. On the one hand, my company and I were hacked, and I know many others have suffered similar fates at the hands of cybercriminals. On the other hand, my company is in one of the hottest tech spaces right now and the exposure we have gotten from my experience with cybersecurity tools and professionals is through the roof.

Due to this exposure, my requests for magazine, TV, and radio interviews have greatly increased. I don't have to spend nearly as much time doing pre-interviews and typing up long e-mails trying to validate my credentials, my expertise, and my company. I can do a quick Google search on all things cybersecurity and usually see my name pop up directly or indirectly related to the story of the day. I have the satisfaction of knowing I have helped people by enabling them to take control of their own security and not live in fear or ignorance.

PART 4

NOTEWORTHY HACKS AND BREACHES

CHAPTER 20

THE TARGET BREACH

LATE IN DECEMBER 2013, NEWS HEADLINES caught my eye regarding the forty million credit card accounts that were stolen from Target retail stores. I knew I would be getting a call for interviews on this one because the Target breach went viral overnight. I realized we had a Target REDcard at home. So how could this have happened on such a grand scale? Big headlines like these are normally reserved for international conflict or dour economic outlooks for entire countries. Now they have become almost commonplace, no longer satisfied with just the financial section of the newspaper. A retail giant or huge entertainment group falls prey to a small band of hackers every other week—or at least, that's what it feels like. I needed to dive deeper to discover the WHO, WHAT, and WHY of this breach on Target.

So I headed straight to a trusted source (and now a friend) for more information: Brian Krebs, a former *Washington Post* reporter and gifted writer. At the time, his blog, *www.KrebsOnSecurity.com*, was celebrating its four-year anniversary and reviewing the big security stories from 2013, including the Adobe and *Washington Post* breaches. But this Target scandal seemed different in both scale and momentum. Every day, new details broke about the stolen accounts: where they were being used and sold, and by whom. Such tenacious reporting by Brian surely accelerated the process and nudged Target to come forward after some time and publicly admit they had, in fact, experienced a serious breach.

It could not have happened at a worse time for Target either, right in the middle of prime-shopping season. Later that night, while glued to the TV watching more news unfold on Target, I talked to my wife about it. She quickly jumped online to make sure no one had run up a Caribbean vacation on our Target REDcard. Fortunately, we were in the clear and saw no activity other than our weekly groceries. In the back of my mind, I was already formulating my talking points, convinced I would be on call for this story as it continued to unfold. There was no doubt this was one of the biggest hacks in history.

Based on prior credit-card breaches, the pattern and sophistication of the Target attack have allegedly pointed the finger to a notorious twenty-two-year-old Ukrainian man who had been repeatedly caught stealing private data within Russia. His identity has been confirmed by several sources—yet as of this writing, there has been no clear evidence connecting him to the breach. From the traces of malware that were found post-breach, it is believed the young hacker was not alone but worked with numerous accomplices who authored the malware. There were sufficient clues left behind that strongly suggested this hacker was behind six other data thefts over the last two years.

How did the cyberhackers actually get into Target during December 2013 to cause one of the most notorious breaches in history? The hackers initially gained access to Target's network by going through a third-party HVAC contractor. It is believed the hackers used login credentials that were directly tied into Target's automated billing/contract proposal system used by third-party vendors. Fazio Mechanical Services, Inc., of Sharpsburg, Pennsylvania, was specifically cited by US Secret Service spokesman Brian Leary, investigator on this specific breach. Target's failing was that it did not secure its third-party vendors and isolate them from accessing its payment systems, which is basically Cybersecurity 101.

The hackers effectively installed credit card malware that captured and relayed customers' private data to three staging servers within the United States so as not to raise red flags before ending in Moscow. On December 2, 2013, the hackers began the massive download of 11 GB of data from the 1,797 US Target stores. This advanced malware was carefully placed on cashier stations throughout Target stores across the country. Exactly two weeks after the forty million compromised credit cards had been stolen, federal investigators warned Target of the massive data breach on December 12, 2013. Target finally took action on December 15, 2013, by removing the malware but it was too late, since the damage was done and the data had already been sent to Moscow.

The customers' account numbers, expiration dates, and secret CVV codes have value in the underground world of the dark web. Hackers typically sell the compromised stolen card information to card counterfeiters who "burn" new credit cards using their own magstripe encoding machines. It's been estimated that somewhere between one and three million of the over forty million stolen credit cards were successfully sold on the black market for on average of $27 each. The hackers successfully generated $53.7 million in income before the credit card companies had the chance to cancel the cards.

Stolen credit card value is dependent upon market conditions, such as supply and demand. If there are millions of available credit cards on the black market (a large supply) then the demand is somewhat diminished. Another important factor is how "fresh" the credit card is. A freshly acquired stolen credit card can fetch from $26 to $45. In comparison, stale, older compromised credit cards may only fetch $8 to $28 each. (Source: *http://krebsonsecurity.com/2014/02/fire-sale-on-cards-stolen-in-target-breach*.) As expected, higher-end cards, such as the American Express Centurion

Card (black card), are worth far more on the black market because their credit limits are significantly higher, allowing cyberthieves to capitalize more returns.

In hindsight, one of the biggest mistakes made after the Target breach was that the issuing banks did not cancel the credit cards promptly enough, which allowed the cyberthieves to quickly sell them at top dollar. Some of the early credit cards were sold for as much as $135 each. Since the Target breach, banks have spent a reported $100 million to reissue 21.8 million new credit cards, accounting for about half the total Target breach. According to *Credit.com*, a Consumers Bankers Association report indicated the final tally to replace the credit and debit cards stolen in the Target breach will exceed $200 million.

Inside Edition and CTV (from Canada, but located in the ABC studio) were the first calls I got the next day. The *Inside Edition* producer said he saw my cybersecurity interviews on the NSA breaches and wanted me on their program immediately to weigh in on the Target debacle. Upon arriving at ABC/CTV studios, I was greeted by security and whisked into the green room to meet the booker who'd arranged the interview. The room was abuzz with fifty people typing away frantically, running, and yelling to each other (much like the show *The Newsroom*). I saw several monitors with the Target logo and heard something to the effect of: "We have that cybersecurity expert here, so maybe we can get him on another segment." The booker called me over to the CTV interview area to get seated with a mic and earpiece in place. There was a quick sound check while I waited and stared at the camera five feet in front of my face. Not seeing who you are talking to is a bit strange, almost as much as the half-second delay from the satellite link, but you adjust after a few times.

The Canadian TV producer greeted me on my earpiece and mentioned I would be live after a few commercials and to standby. Just then, the managing editor of ABC News thanked me for coming and asked if I could do two more interviews after my CTV appearance to be used for their New York and Washington, DC, affiliates. Before I could answer, my iPhone vibrated with a text to head over to BloombergTV after my interview for the live 3:00 p.m. *Street Smart* show—on the breaking Target story, of course.

Someone silenced the chaos-filled room when she shouted, "We are live in thirty seconds!" All eyes were now on me. Thirty seconds quickly became, "You are live in ten seconds." I glanced to my right and to my left as employees lined up to watch their office cubicle transform into a live-interview backdrop before all our eyes. The blinding LED lights flooded my face as the sound kicked in, and I heard myself being introduced.

At this moment, my internal switch clicked to ON, and for the next few minutes I become the cybersecurity expert. It is important to be a good listener in interviews but more important to effectively convey concise, pointed answers to real questions. Television viewers and listeners do not just want to hear opinions; they also want you to relate to and understand their feelings and concerns. Viewers are pretty smart but have a short attention span, so large headlines broken down into smaller pieces of information work well—or they will simply get their news from a source that saves them that extra ten seconds.

They want headlines that answer two focused questions: First, how did this happen? And second, what can I do as a consumer to protect my family and myself? I try to answer these questions even if the interviewer does not specifically ask them. So even when it is no more than a prearranged problem/solution discussion, I try to directly appeal to the viewers by relaying a short personal example of how the specific breach affected me, my business, or my family. I know when I'm watching the news, I tend to trust and respect the guests I can best relate to, so I keep that in mind during my own interviews. Knowing your subject well and keeping on top of the daily news is almost as important as conversing with others about it to also get a sense of what is on the viewers' minds. Being able to strike a chord with viewers is important, too. After my first few TV interviews, I was encouraged to talk "tech," but put it in everyday terms that viewers can understand. I can relate to this advice. When I go to a doctor, I can't stand the way they carelessly rattle off meaningless acronyms. I do not speak medical jargon, nor do I want to learn it. If I ask them to explain it in layman's terms and they respond in a condescending manner, I know it's time for a second opinion and a new doctor.

Just when I thought the dust was settling from the massive Target hack, I learned it was actually heating up. The next day I was booked on CNBC's *Street Signs*. I was quickly learning that when I am called to these interviews, I am often in good company with great business talent, making for great networking opportunities. At CNBC, I was in the makeup chair and set up for sound, then we were quickly directed to our seats and respective cameras. One of the experts got a bit panicked, wondering which camera to look at. I leaned in and said, "Don't worry. Just stare straight ahead until they address you. After that, look at the anchors and ignore the cameras, as they know how to make it look good." A few dozen interviews ago, I wondered about the very same thing, but you learn quickly.

Two days later, the Target hack was still unfolding. My publicist called me at home that night and told me I had a 4:45 a.m. pickup to the city—for a 6:00 a.m. morning show on CNN called *New Day*. Chris Cuomo, Kate Bolduan, and Michaela Pereira would be interviewing me. I had never been on CNN before, so I quickly gathered my talking points. Arriving on the set was awesome; CNN is a high-tech studio with a world-class pedigree and before I knew it, I was sitting among the anchors and the interview had begun. I thought I would be with a panel of other experts, but in this case I was CNN's go-to cybersecurity expert at this moment.

For me, the Target breach was a crash course in television interviewing, and it was great exposure. Even though I had my first television interview back in 2011 on Fox News, the Target breach ushered cybersecurity center stage and I was able to effectively ride the wave that has lead to so many additional things, such as this book. Target was such a massive, widespread breach and everyone was talking about it, and the calls have been coming in ever since.

Since the Target breach, I am continually asked how the breach happened. At the end of the day it was Target's responsibility to ensure that all customers' credit card data and credentials were secure. The cyberhackers would have not been successful if Target had employed proper network segmentation at the onset. The cyberhackers exploited the weakest point and left Target holding the bag.

The Target breach set a precedent for how not to handle damage control post-breach. Since they did not report the breach in a timely manner, their customer base punished them by avoiding their stores for fear their credit cards might be compromised. Target's stock took a hit as shareholder confidence was tested. Eventually, Target's CEO was ousted, and its stellar brand will be marred for years to come. The aftermath of any major cyberbreach is nearly impossible to translate into hard dollar figures; so many parties are involved and it will be many years before all the facts unfold.

——————

QUICK TIP: When you are shopping in Target or any other retailer, use caution when checking out. I prefer using cash or my Visa credit card with chip-and-pin technology. The additional layer of security is added when entering a PIN manually.

CHAPTER 21

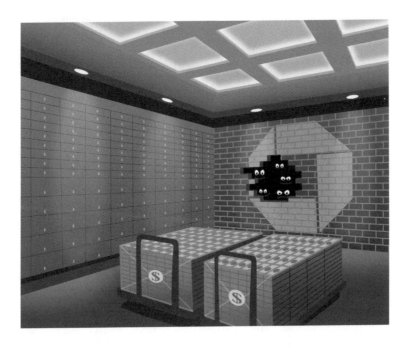

AND THE BREACHES KEEP COMING (JP MORGAN CHASE BREACH)

TARGET WILL CERTAINLY GO DOWN as the first noteworthy retail cyberbreach in history. The media has analyzed Target inside and out, and uses it as a gauge for other breaches. But just when I thought nothing could come close to Target, I learned JP Morgan Chase was hacked in the summer of 2014. Now that I have some recognition in the cybersecurity space, I am often alerted about breaches from friends, family, and business associates the moment they hear the news. In fact, when the JP Morgan breach hit, I received many texts, e-mails, and calls asking me just what happened.

To all my associates and friends, I would like to take a moment to say THANK YOU, as I strongly believe to stay safe, we all need to communicate effectively and share information. Of course, right after I first heard the news, I rolled up my sleeves and started to absorb all the information I could on JP Morgan Chase and the breach details that were still unfolding. I like to find the missing angle that gets lost or blurred by the sensationalism of many cyberhacks.

JP Morgan Chase's immense cyberdata breach resulted in over seventy-six million customers having their personal data compromised, including their names, phone numbers, addresses, and e-mail addresses. Also not to be overlooked in this breach were seven million small businesses that had their data compromised, as well. This unprecedented breach was the largest intrusion of an American bank, ever. I quickly realized that to have the level of access to this much sensitive data required some compromise from the inside.

Typically, when I delve into a breach I like to read every source I can, to wrap my head around the story. Some news outlets take liberties and jump the gate too quickly in the race to a headline. As with all breaches, many experts start speculating before collecting all of the evidence. Case in point: JP Morgan's security experts and the FBI suspected a sophisticated adversary was behind the breach. Many media outlets jumped on this theory and suspected the attack was retaliation against economic sanctions levied by the United States and its allies in response to Russia's policies in Ukraine. However, by mid-October 2014, that theory began to unravel, and the FBI officially ruled out the Russian government as a culprit.

At the time, many also were quick to discount this breach because no financial information had been compromised, and the hackers only stole customers' contact information. I certainly disagreed. As I discussed on a *Street Smart* interview, cyberhackers generally take as much information as possible and use it for multiple purposes, such as exploiting individuals in well-crafted phishing attacks or selling the packaged information to other thieves with identity theft in mind. When thieves put together stolen personal identification, they will next apply for credit in the victim's name to spend a lot of money quickly, incur debt, and finally disappear, leaving the victim to clean up the mess.

The other *Street Smart* guest was TeleSign's CEO, Steve Jillings, who made a brilliant point about the hacking community doing a phenomenally great job of collaborating and sharing hacked information—something the cybersecurity community all too frequently fails to do itself. I wholeheartedly agree that there is no effective and safe means yet to share information between the public and private sectors, whereas cybercriminals generously share information, tools, and techniques that other hackers will then customize for the next focused attack. It's a culture not too different from the old "home-brew" computer clubs in the 1970s and '80s.

The banking industry invests more capital into security than almost any other industry. It also effectively applies best practices throughout the banking sector better than most industries. But the second your money is compromised at a bank, you will always think twice before putting more money in that particular institution. In fact, the manner in which a breached company responds and informs its customers tells a lot about a corporation and sets the stage for its current and future customers.

All businesses are potential targets for a cyberbreach, but what separates a good company from a bad one is the manner in which it handles the situation and inform its customers, shareholders, and employees. Overall, JP Morgan Chase reacted swiftly and informed its customer base much faster than Target did. Perhaps it's an apples-to-oranges comparison or the fact that Target was completely blindsided by the first big breach, but I can't help but think how differently things could have worked out in Target's favor had it simply owned the situation and was transparent from the start.

JP Morgan Chase CEO, Jamie Dimon, responded to questions quickly and assured anxious listeners that only customer contact data was compromised and no customer financial accounts were breached. While JP Morgan Chase was already spending over $250 million a year on security, Dimon pledged to double its cybersecurity investment over the next five years. He also assured investors that multiple layers of security would be deployed to protect the privacy of its customers. Cybersecurity and services are among the fastest-growing business segments in the United States, and this is precisely the reason why.

When a breach hits, everyone is screaming for a quick and speedy resolution. It is hard to imagine a price too high for security measures that not only fix the problem but assuage the public's fear and wariness.

We will never fully understand all the facets of the JP Morgan Chase breach, but one takeaway is that the implementation of layered security and best practices from the top down and everything in between is the best way to ensure security (it's not always the amount of money in the security budget). It is likely that if JP Morgan Chase had installed a simple security fix to an overlooked server in its vast network, the breach may have never happened. On August 5, 2014, Hold Security first reported the breach to the New York Times, tracing data stolen from the JP Morgan Chase's Corporate Challenge website back to Russian hackers. JP Morgan sponsors a series of charitable races run by an outside vendor, in which the race participants' login credentials were intercepted and stolen. From there, passwords and login combinations were tested by hackers across ninety of the bank's servers.

We may never get the full story, but it's clear that security was not up to par in several areas where JP Morgan's servers and outside vendors crossed paths. It's easy to play Monday-morning quarterback by saying they should have invested more money in security and caught the breach sooner. During an interview on Al Jazeera America in New York City, I mentioned that cyberhackers always look to exploit the backdoor vulnerability first. Hence, if they didn't initially find a means into the bank's secure server, they would keep looking for another hole to exploit. Weak pass-words provide easy remote access into a company's server, thereby allowing third-party access to anyone. Instead of these third-party companies getting atten-tion and pressure from the security community, we find the hackers getting all the attention and acclaim from the security community, the media, and fellow hackers. Until this media misdirection is fixed, hackers will con-tinue to exploit security weaknesses among third-party vendors and ultimately their larger customers like JP Morgan Chase.

CYBER STAT: Gartner (a well-respected information tech-nology research firm) estimates that governments and companies across the globe will spend $77 billion on cyberprotection in 2015, and this spending will increase by eight percent per year for the next decade.

CHAPTER 22

iCLOUD CYBERHACK: NUDE CELEBRITY PHOTOS EXPOSED

THIS ONE WILL CERTAINLY GO DOWN in the history books as one of the most scandalous hacks since it involved over one hundred celebrities' nude photos stolen from their personal iCloud accounts and posted on multiple websites on August 31, 2014. In some instances, the photos were Tweeted or posted freely to websites like 4chan. In other cases, downloaded photos and videos were held for ransom or sold to the highest bidders. Most of the postings were quickly pulled from the websites as celebrities frantically removed and deleted photos and changed their iCloud account passwords. This was a clear violation of privacy, and many victimized celebrities spoke out against their perpetrators and even the public as accomplices in these crimes.

I received a call from *Inside Edition* just as the story was breaking. This show has a large audience of people who follow the celebrities and their scandalous lives and careers. When I asked what time they wanted me in the studio, they said NOW. There was no time for a trip to their studios, so they told me to FaceTime them on my iPhone in one minute. This helped me appreciate the importance of keeping on top of the latest breach details. I had just read the breaking headlines that morning so I was well aware of the scandal details and more importantly the technical details. As usual, the media outlets were focused on Apple as the host, victim, and accessory to the crime; however, a little detective work revealed this was not the case.

When my iPhone rang, I was speaking with *Inside Edition* producer Tyler Woods, who wanted me to comment on how the hackers could've gotten in from the tech angle. I shared some information on the hacker known as Bluntmastermind who uses a program called iBrute (a free application found on Github). The iBrute Python script (which is a general-purpose, high-level programming language) allows a hacker to use a target's iCloud username (often their e-mail account). The e-mail account itself is easy to obtain or even guess because it is typically a person's name followed by @icloud.com. From there, iBrute will start trying password after password, thousands per second, and alerts the hacker when a password works. In this case, Bluntmastermind took advantage of a security flaw in Apple's online backup service for iCloud, also used in the "Find My iPhone" application.

Many online services lock a user out after several unsuccessful attempts to log in. However, prior to this hack, Apple's iCloud and Find My iPhone allowed endless login attempts (in some cases, Find My iPhone passwords were also weak and even reused for that same user's iCloud account). This was a terrible oversight on Apple's part, and post-breach Apple immediately fixed this vulnerability by limiting logins to a maximum of three attempts. But the damage was already done. With unlimited guesses, a computer program like iBrute can generate and test hundreds of thousands of potential passwords until the account is hacked. This is called a "brute force attack."

The fundamental security problem with all the hacked celebrity iCloud accounts was the passwords were all weak. The celebrities should not be blamed for taking nude selfies. They should also not be blamed for trusting iCloud security with their personal data. However, they should take part of the blame for using weak passwords to access their iCloud accounts. We have all taken shortcuts with too-easy-to-guess passwords from time to time, but we also should typically use a level of password security that is matched to what we want to secure. If these celebrities were truly devastated by the attack on their privacy, perhaps they should have valued their privacy more by implementing difficult-to-guess passwords. Remember, there is a social component that must be used in conjunction with a program like iBrute. This hacking software makes many guesses quickly, but the guesses can only be as good as what the hacker feeds it. This is usually the contents of the entire English dictionary and, in this particular case, social-media clues scraped off the celebrities' websites—meaning the celebrities locked the gate but left the key right under the most conspicuous rock right next to the locked gate.

This gathering of social media and failed-password attempts occurred over many months without any of the victims realizing they were being hacked, or even that an attempt was being made. This is where Apple must take some of the blame, because if cyberthieves are not locked out after three attempts, users will not be notified so they could never have known they were being hacked. There are still many cloud services available that are susceptible to this type of brute force attack. The difference here is that Apple is a brand that both consumers and celebrities flock to for personal use.

Metadata in selfies and celebrity photos quickly reveal that an iPhone took the picture. It's not a stretch to assume this iPhone user also uses iCloud to store this and all their private photos. People assume it is safe, but many celebrities are targets for hackers looking for quick glory or profits. When a hacker can safely assume a celebrity is using iCloud services, it's only a matter of time before they can piece together the right clues, allowing them to penetrate that user's account. Then, couple that with security flaws allowing limitless login attempts and you get the iCloud hacking scandal. It was inevitable on some level.

Password reuse across multiple accounts is extremely common and a huge danger. So why did the celebrities reuse their passwords? For the same reasons most people do: they are easier to remember. Keep in mind that celebrities are often traveling for prolonged periods of time, and remembering many long, complex passwords can be a challenge. Perhaps they have handlers or assistants, but unless those assistants are well versed in best security practices, chances are they make the same mistakes as their celebrity employers. If the victims, in fact, had strong passwords, they would most likely never have been compromised.

None of the celebrities whose iCloud accounts were hacked had implemented an additional layer of security called two-factor (or multifactor) authentication. Two-factor authentication requires you to enter your password and another verification step, such as a PIN texted to your cell phone. That is another security change Apple recently began requiring of all new iCloud accounts, and one that would have surely stopped the hackers cold. I always encourage people to consider layers of security to thwart cyberthieves who continue focusing on the easiest of targets.

Often, when a login prompt notices that an IP address is not the one commonly associated with the account, it will issue a randomized security challenge question. With famous people, a host of information is readily available to hackers. They pay publicists and agents to make the celebrities' lives an open book. For example, if a hacker trying to gain access to a celebrity's account was asked a security challenge question, such as: "What high school did you attend?" a Google search can find the answer in .58 seconds. There is an abundant amount of information about celebrities and their lives on social media, so most of the challenge question answers are actually easily obtainable.

I recommend that everyone, not just celebrities, use a complex, strong password to answer your security challenge questions instead of honestly answering them. This would be virtually impossible for anyone except you to know, and adds a valuable layer of security. So instead of providing the high school you actually went to, use a unique, strong password, such as Xg45k*lq@iqdS!#.

The iCloud hacks gained wide spread notoriety when Bluntmastermind posted the stolen nude photos on 4chan, which is an anonymous, public Internet bulletin board where people can access content, such as pictures and videos, without registering. Over the years, many 4chan users used the site to initiate pranks and share unsavory or illegally obtained content. After the iCloud-stolen nude photos were posted, 4chan announced it would enforce the Digital Millennium Copyright Act (DMCA) policy that allows content owners to remove material illegally shared on the site. Further, this would also ban all registered users who repeatedly posted the stolen photos. The iCloud hacking story continues to resonate among users and security experts. If you play word association with most people and say "iCloud," many will come back at you with "nude photos" or "hacked celebrities" or even "Jennifer Lawrence." Or just try Googling the first few letters of each to see what I mean. As this story unfolded I received calls and had several additional interviews on CCTV America, Arise TV, and *On Point* with Tomi Lahren to weigh in on the iCloud hacks.

———————

QUICK TIP: Don't store your nude photos on the cloud, no matter how good you might think they look. Use a strong password for all cloud data storage.

CHAPTER 23

SONY CYBERBREACHES

THE MOST RECENT SONY CYBERBREACH on November 24, 2014, is considered the first major attack against a US corporation. However, that breach was the latest in a line of security breaches at Sony that stretches back to 2011. Many companies are attacked just because they are vulnerable targets, but Sony seems to have raised a special ire in the hacktivist community. Looking back on the timeline of the company's major security breaches provides some insight as to why Sony has been an ongoing target for so many years.

In 2005, Sony began producing audio CDs with intrusive digital rights management (DRM) software included on the disc. If someone loaded the disc into their computer, it automatically installed a rootkit that made changes to the computer's operating system and prevented it from copying the CD. The disc also installed software that would track the user's listening habits and made the computer vulnerable to a host of hackers. Worst of all, there was no easy way to uninstall it.

Another event that ticked off the hacking community occurred in 2010, when a well-known hacker named George Hotz broke the copy protection on PlayStation 3, making it possible for users to play pirated games. Sony took the hacker to court, and even got a judge to order the company hosting the hacker's website to turn over server logs as a means to identify the IP addresses of people who accessed his site. The same month Sony settled with Hotz out of court, the first major attack occurred.

Back in April 2011, there was an attack on the PlayStation Network (PSN) perpetrated by the "hacktivist" group called Anonymous. Personal details of over seventy-seven million PSN users were stolen and the PSN service was knocked offline for twenty-three days. As a result, this breach cost Sony a minimum of $171 million.

Then, in May 2011, there was a focused attack on Sony Online Entertainment by unknown perpetrators. The personal details and credit card information of 24.6 million Sony customers were stolen. The following month, Sony Pictures Entertainment was attacked. This the hack was perpetrated by the hacktivist group called LulzSec. The personal details of over one million accounts were stolen this time, but it didn't sound like a difficult hack to pull off. The hackers claimed passwords were stored in plain unencrypted text and were easy to find.

More recently, in August 2014, a DDoS attack on PSN was perpetrated along with other online gaming networks. This time, it was initiated by hacktivist group known as Lizard Squad. Fortunately, no customer data was compromised during that attack. Lizard Squad actually called in a bomb threat against American Airlines that forced a jet carrying a Sony executive out of the sky. Attacks like these are very concerning, as they flirt with the public's safety—often with unknown consequences. It also emboldens other hackers to try their hand at adding chaos into both the digital and real world.

In November 2014, Sony Pictures Entertainment was hacked again; this time it was a highly publicized, widespread takedown of Sony's internal network, first believed to have been launched by the hacker group called Guardians of Peace (or GoP). The hackers concentrated on releasing embarrassing, damaging information about Sony and its executives. Details slowly came out gleaned from executive e-mails about pay disparities and personal feuds with actors, actresses, and employees. This resulted in a corporate nightmare for Sony as it went into damage control not to lose employees, contracts, and the insulted celebrities. For weeks, the hackers held a huge trove of stolen data and messages over Sony, releasing the most damaging bits day by day.

In December 2014, the FBI sent a confidential notice about the cyberattack on Sony Pictures Entertainment to security staff at some large US companies. While the notice did not specify Sony Pictures specifically, it provided details on how the hack was pulled off. It also warned that data destroyed by the malware could be impossible or just too costly to recover by using current forensic data retrieval methods. The malware overwrote data and destroyed master boot records on the servers' hard drives. Details on how the attack began are also sketchy, but these types of attacks usually start with inside help or a successful phishing attempt. Once hackers find their way into the system, they can move through the network swiftly.

The damage inflicted caused Sony to take more than a week after the hack attack just to get back online. While some services were restored quickly, others remained offline for some time. And even after services were fully restored, many Sony employees continued to avoid e-mails and other forms of digital messaging for fear the hackers would strike again. Business over the phone and in person made a brief but strong comeback as a result of the widespread corporate panic. The hackers claimed to have stolen and erased (on Sony's end) up to one hundred terabytes of data from Sony's servers. A short time after the attack, digital copies of five unreleased Sony Pictures movies were leaked to illegal file sharing sites, although it's not entirely clear if the films were stolen by the hackers or leaked by other means.

A website run by the North Korean government blasted Sony Pictures for creating the action comedy called *The Interview* with a plot centered around an assassination attempt of North Korean leader Kim Jong Un. The state-controlled media called the film "an act of war," and messages from the hackers who claimed responsibility for the attack lauded Sony's decision to ultimately pull the film before its theatrical premiere. *The Interview* was not one of the films leaked, but it quickly became a scapegoat and even motivation for the hackers' actions. Meanwhile, the malware the FBI warned US companies about was reportedly written in Korean and has similarities to malware used in an attack on South Korean banks and television broadcasters in 2013. The two countries are hostile neighbors, and South Korea is a frequent target of North Korean hacking attacks. Sony Pictures has hired the Mandiant division of FireEye, a security consulting firm, to assist with the investigation and eventual recovery of stolen data. Both companies and the FBI continue to pursue the matter.

To the surprise of practically no one, the FBI officially announced the involvement of the North Korean government in the hack on Sony Pictures Entertainment. While the announcement stated it could not list all of the reasons for the link due to the need to protect "sensitive sources and methods," it listed several links that will be familiar to many. There was infrastructure associated with IP addresses known to be used by the North Korean government, which communicated with computers with IP addresses written directly into the malware used in the attack.

The FBI report also expressed concern that the attack was aimed at a private entity not connected to government activity, since most officially sanctioned hacking is limited to targeting foreign governments or their contractors.

While the North Korean government continues to maintain it was not behind the attack, President Obama stated, "We've got no indication that North Korea was acting in conjunction with another country." Even though North Korea is a nation of poverty with very limited Internet access and the citizens are practically isolated from the rest of the world, the government maintains a cyberespionage department called Bureau 121. Unlike most countries that engage in cyberespionage, Bureau 121 will target any public or private entity that raises the ire of the North Korean government.

According to North Korean defectors, positions in Bureau 121 are highly sought after, and the people admitted are hand-picked and trained at an age as young as seventeen. There are reportedly 1,800 cyber-warriors in the North Korean elite military group, giving North Korea the ability to wage cyberwarfare at a level far beyond what most third-world countries are capable of. In fact, North Korea considers cyberattacks an effective method of making up for its lack of traditional military strength.

As with the other major cyberhacks, I was on the radar of many media groups and the calls started coming in from the moment the breach occurred. I had numerous interviews on Arise TV, CCTV in New York City at the NASDAQ building, and CCTV in DC. I was also interviewed on the Sony breach for numerous articles.

As the story unfolded, I was able to provide regular updates to Benzinga online and Yahoo! News, where I am quoted on all of the developments.

CHAPTER 24

OFFICE OF PERSONNEL MANAGEMENT: THE GREATEST GOVERNMENT HACK EVER

WHEN THE OFFICE OF PERSONNEL MANAGEMENT (OPM) was hacked in June 2015 and some four million current and former US government employee records had been accessed, there was immediate concern. From mid-2015 onward, more updates and revelations emerged as we started to get a sense of how big this hack actually was. In all, the number of people whose records were exposed grew from 4.2 million to 21.5

million—which is nearly seven percent of the entire US population.

The breach affected a lot more people than anyone could have imagined; in fact, anyone who has applied for a security clearance in the past fifteen years was compromised. OPM and the Defense Department confirmed that troops, civilians, and contractors subjected to background checks since 2000 were exposed in the breach, which the Obama administration has pinned on China.

Many, including me, wondered what had actually been hacked. I learned that Social Security numbers, residency and education information, employment history, health information, and criminal and financial histories were all compromised. Not only had private individuals' information been hacked, but also notes and data obtained by investigators in interviews, as well as personal information about immediate family members. The breach affected security-clearance applicants, along with nearly two million spouses and cohabitants.

Not surprisingly, as with all cyberbreaches, OPM said it would provide credit monitoring and fraud insurance to anyone, including cohabitants and spouses, affected by the breach for three years, but that timeframe is not set in stone and perhaps will be extended.

If you were a victim of this hack, there are a few things you can immediately do—starting with updating all your passwords. Officials say it's a good idea to avoid using birthdays, names, or addresses that could be easily gleaned from your security-clearance applications, as it's safe to assume that information is no longer secure. You should also be on the lookout for phishing scams.

It's generally a bad idea to click on URLs sent to you in an e-mail from a dubious source, or a source that may be trying to pass itself off as a legitimate entity like a bank. It's also a bad idea to give out any personal information solicited via e-mail, because that is not how legitimate businesses behave.

The Obama administration has not laid out a clear response to the hack, but officials have said economic sanctions against China are on the table. The problem, though, is that in order to levy sanctions, the White House has to prove beyond a shadow of a doubt that the hack was sponsored by the Chinese state, and that's a tall order. The administration has shown a willingness to wage cyberwar in the past, though. In 2009, it unleashed the world's first cyberweapon on Iran's nuclear enterprise. The so-called "Stuxnet virus" wreaked havoc on Iran's nuclear developments and ushered in a new era of cyberwarfare. The administration was also implicated as a source of widespread Internet outages in North Korea following the Sony cyberattack that was blamed on the rogue Asian nation.

IN CONCLUSION

MANY PEOPLE ASK ME IF I THINK WE WILL EVER BEAT the cyberhackers. With confidence, I can say that it is not about winning or losing as much as it is about *not* giving up. Security is everyone's business, and we must come together to combat the threat of evil and apathy in order to share information.

I hope that you can benefit from my misfortunes of being *Hacked Again*. Perhaps my mistakes will enable you to strengthen your cyberdefenses and not become another victim. I'll leave you now with my parting words from every episode of my two-minute cybersecurity briefing podcasts: Stay Safe.

GLOSSARY

Anonymous: A group of hacktivist entities known for well-publicized publicity stunts and DDoS attacks against government, religious, and corporate websites.

Antivirus software: A program that monitors a computer or network to detect or identify major types of malicious code and to prevent or contain malware incidents, sometimes by removing or neutralizing the malicious code.

AP (Access Point): AP is a device that allows wireless devices to connect to a wired network using Wi-Fi or related standards.

Attack: An attempt to gain unauthorized access to system services, resources, or information, or an attempt to compromise system integrity.

Backdoor: In a computer system, a method of bypassing normal authentication, securing unauthorized remote access to a computer

Bitcoin: Innovative payment network. A type of digital currency in which encryption techniques are used to regulate the generation of units of currency and verify the transfer of funds, operating independently of a central bank. Many Bitcoin transactions are associated with illegal dark web activity, but not all. Payment by Bitcoins allows cyberthieves to remain completely anonymous.

Blacklist: A list of entities that are blocked or denied privileges or access.

Black hat: A hacker who uses his or her abilities for malicious or selfish purposes.

Bot: A computer connected to the Internet that has been surreptitiously/secretly compromised with malicious logic to perform activities under the command and control of a remote administrator.

Botnet: A collection of computers compromised by malicious code and controlled across a network.

Brute force attack: This type of attack aims at being the simplest kind of method to gain access to a site: it tries usernames and passwords, over and over again, until it gets in.

Cipher: A cryptographic algorithm.

Chargeback: When a cardholder disputes a charge with the bank (the "issuing bank"), the bank may reverse the payment and refund the cardholder, after an investigation.

Cloud computing: A model for enabling on-demand network access to a shared pool of configurable computing capabilities or resources (e.g., networks, servers, storage, applications, and services) that can be rapidly provisioned and released with minimal management effort or service provider interaction.

Critical infrastructure: The systems and assets, whether physical or virtual, so vital to society that the incapacity or destruction of such may have a debilitating impact on the security, economy, public health or safety, environment, or any combination of these matters.

Cryptography: The use of mathematical techniques to provide security services, such as confidentiality, data integrity, entity authentication, and data origin authentication.

Cybersecurity: The activity or process, ability or capability, or state whereby information and communications systems and the information contained therein are protected from and/or defended against damage, unauthorized use or modification, or exploitation.

Dark web: The portion of World Wide Web content not indexed by standard search engines that is generally attributed to hacking and illegal cyber activities.

Data breach: The unauthorized movement or disclosure of sensitive information to a party, usually outside the organization, that is not authorized to have or see the information.

Data theft: The deliberate or intentional act of stealing information.

DDoS (Distributed Denial of Service): An attack that prevents or impairs the authorized use of information system resources or services.

Decipher: To convert enciphered text to plain text by means of a cryptographic system.

Decode: To convert encoded text to plain text by means of a code.

Decrypt: A generic term encompassing decode and decipher.

Deep web: The portion of World Wide Web content that is not indexed by standard search engines; generally attributed to hacking and illegal cyber activities.

DMCA: Digital Millennium Copyright Act

Encryption: The process of transforming plaintext into cipher text.

FCC (Federal Communications Commission): An independent agency of the United States government, created by Congressional statute to regulate interstate communications by radio, television, wire, satellite, and cable in all fifty states, the District of Columbia, and US territories.

FTC (Federal Trade Commission): An independent agency of the United States government. The principal mission of the FTC is the promotion of consumer protection.

Firewall: A capability to limit network traffic between networks and/or information systems.

Hack: An unauthorized attempt to gain access to an information system.

Hacker: An unauthorized user who attempts to or gains access to an information system.

Hacktivist: A computer hacker whose activity is aimed at promoting a social or political cause.

Hashing: A process of applying a mathematical algorithm against a set of data to produce a numeric value (a "hash value") that represents the data.

Incident response plan: A set of predetermined and documented procedures to detect and respond to a cyber incident.

Industrial control system: An information system used to control industrial processes such as manufacturing, product handling, production, and distribution, or to control infrastructure assets.

Insider threat: A person or group of persons within an organization who pose a potential risk through violating security policies.

Intrusion detection: The process and methods for analyzing information from networks and information systems to determine whether a security breach or security violation has occurred.

IoT (The Internet of Things): Provides unique identifiers and the ability to transfer data over a network without requiring human-to-human or human-to-computer interaction.

IPS (Intrusion Prevention System): A network security/ threat-prevention technology that examines network traffic flows to detect and prevent vulnerability exploits.

ISP (Internet Service Provider): An organization that provides services for accessing and using the Internet.

Key: The numerical value used to control cryptographic operations, such as decryption, encryption, signature generation, or signature verification.

Keylogger: Software or hardware that tracks keystrokes and keyboard events, usually surreptitiously/secretly, to monitor actions by the user of an information system.

Lizard Squad: A black hat hacking group known mainly for their claims of distributed denial of service (DDoS) attacks, primarily to disrupt gaming-related services.

Malicious code: Program code intended to perform an unauthorized function or process that will have adverse impact on the confidentiality, integrity, or availability of an information system.

Malware: Software that compromises the operation of a system by performing an unauthorized function or process.

MITM (Man-in-the-Middle): Using false digital credentials or certificates to fool a device or user into thinking it is communicating directly with the intended site by rerouting Internet traffic through another server.

MoneyPak: MoneyPak is a stored-value card provided by Green Dot Corp. MoneyPak is typically purchased with cash at a retailer, then used to fund prepaid debit cards or online wallet services like PayPal.

NFC (Near Field Communication): A technology that enables mobile phones and electronic devices to establish radio communications with each other by bringing them in close proximity of each other (typically fewer than four inches). NFC is a short-range wireless communication where the antenna used is much smaller than the wavelength of the carrier signal. Although the communication range of NFC is limited to a few centimeters, NFC alone does not ensure secure communications because they are susceptible to relay attacks.

Null Route: A null route is a network route that goes nowhere. Matching packets are dropped and basically ignored rather than forwarded, acting as a kind of very limited firewall.

Onion Routing: A technique for anonymous commu-

-nication over a computer network where messages are put in layers of encryption, similar to layers of the vegetable onion.

Password: A string of characters (letters, numbers, and other symbols) used to authenticate an identity or to verify access authorization.

Pen test: A colloquial term for penetration test or penetration testing.

Penetration testing: An evaluation methodology whereby assessors search for vulnerabilities and attempt to circumvent the security features of a network and/or information system.

Phishing: A digital form of social engineering to deceive individuals into providing sensitive information.

PLC (Programmable Logic Controllers): A digital computer used for automation of typically industrial electrome-chanical processes, such as control of machinery.

Privacy: The assurance that the confidentiality of, and access to, certain information about an entity is protected.

Private key: A cryptographic key that must be kept confidential and is used to enable the operation of an asymmetric (public key) cryptographic algorithm.

Public key: A cryptographic key that may be widely published and is used to enable the operation of an asymmetric (public key) cryptographic algorithm.

Ransomware: A strain of malware that restricts access to a computer that it infects, and the hacker demands a ransom to be paid to the originator of the malware (the hacker) in order for the restriction to be removed. The computer data is encrypted until the ransom is paid (usually in Bitcoins) in which a "key" is provided to decrypt the data.

Recovery: The activities after an incident or event to restore essential services and operations in the short and medium term and fully restore all capabilities in the longer term.

Risk Analysis: The systematic examination of the components and characteristics of risk.

Rooted: The process of allowing users of smartphones running Android mobile operating system to attain privileged control over Android subsystems.

Rootkit: A set of software tools with administrator-level access privileges installed on an information system and designed to hide the presence of the tools, maintain the access privileges, and conceal the activities conducted by the tools.

SCIF (Sensitive Compartmented Information Facility):

Location where the United States military processes sensitive classified information. Access is normally limited to those with clearance.

Security policy: A rule or set of rules that governs the use of an organization's information and services to a level of acceptable risk, and the means for protecting the organization's information assets.

Situational awareness: Comprehending information about the current and developing security posture and risks, based on information gathered, observation and analysis, and knowledge or experience.

Script kiddie: An unskilled individual who uses scripts or programs developed by others to attack computer systems and networks, and deface websites.

SMS (Short Message Service): A texting messaging service used on mobile communication devices.

Social engineering: An effective tactic hackers employ to play against human interaction and often involves tricking individuals to break normal security procedures.

Spam: Undesired or unsolicited electronic messages. These are illegal e-mail messages. Electronic spam came from the original Spam that was a canned pork meat product.

Spider: Type of web crawler that is an Internet bot and browses the web for the purpose of web indexing.

Spoofing: Faking the sending address of a transmission to gain illegal [unauthorized] entry into a secure system.

Spyware: Software that is secretly or surreptitiously installed into an information system without the knowledge of the system user or owner.

Surface web: The portion of the World Wide Web that is readily available to everyone and searchable with standard web search engines. As of June 14, 2015, Google's index of the surface web contained about 14.5 billion pages.

Threat: A circumstance or event that has or indicates the potential to exploit vulnerabilities and to adversely impact (create adverse consequences for) organizational operations, organizational assets (including information and information systems), individuals, other organizations, or society.

Threat agent: An individual, group, organization, or government that conducts or has the intent to conduct detrimental activities.

TOR (The Onion Router): Free software designed to make it possible for users to surf the Internet anonymously so their activities and location cannot be discovered by government agencies, corporations, or anyone else.

Trojan horse: A type of malware program that is non-self replicating and contains malicious code that upon execution carries out actions determined by the nature of the Trojan. Trojan horses are used to harm computer systems and often cause a loss and/or theft of data.

Two-factor authentication: An extra layer of security known as "multifactor authentication" that requires not only a password and username but also something that only that user has on him or her, or has immediate accessibility to.

Virus: A malware program that, when executed, replicates by inserting copies of itself into other computer programs, data files, or the boot sector of the hard drive. Viruses usually perform some type of harmful activity on infected computers, such as stealing hard disk space or CPU time, accessing private information, corrupting data, spamming their contacts, logging their keystrokes, or even rendering the computer useless.

Vulnerability: A characteristic or specific weakness that renders an organization or asset (such as information or an information system) open to exploitation by a given threat or susceptible to a given hazard.

Wi-Fi: A local area wireless computer networking technology allowing electronic devices to connect using 2.4 GHz & 5 GHz license free spectrum Industrial Scientific Medical (ISM) bands. Also commonly referred to as WLAN.

White hat: Hackers who use their abilities to identify security weaknesses in systems in a way that will allow the systems' owners to fix the weakness.

Whitelist: A list of entities that are considered trustworthy and are granted access or privileges.

Worm: A standalone computer program that has the ability to replicate itself and spread to other computers. A worm is spread through a computer network, but it does not need to attach itself to another computer program, as a virus does.

ABOUT THE AUTHOR

SCOTT N. SCHOBER is a cybersecurity and wireless technology expert, author, and President/CEO of Berkeley Varitronics Systems (BVS), a forty-year-old New Jersey-based, family-owned company. BVS is a leading provider of advanced wireless solutions and products for multinational telecommunications and security markets around the world. Since the beginning of Scott's BVS tenure in 1989, the company's product line of wireless test and security instruments has increased to over one hundred products, with a core focus on Wi-Fi, Cellular, WiMAX, LTE, and advanced radio devices. As an experienced software engineer, Scott has developed cellular test instruments used for measuring, optimizing, and plotting signal coverage, primarily for the initial cellular buildout throughout the United States. Scott's recent focus has been development of cell-phone detection tools used to enforce a "no-cell-phone policy" in various markets, including government, corporate, military, educational, correctional, and law enforcement. Thousands of these security tools have been deployed throughout every state in the country and around the world.

Scott is a highly sought-after cybersecurity expert for media appearances and commentary, as well as technical speaking engagements. Recent media appearances include Bloomberg TV, Canadian TV News, One America Network, and Arise TV, where he is a regular cybersecurity expert and contributor. Scott has also made numerous appearances on Fox Business Channel, Fox

News, *CBS Morning Show*, ABC, Al Jazeera America, CCTV America, *Inside Edition*, MSNBC, CNBC, CNN, PIX11, The Blaze, and more to weigh in on the largest retail, corporate, government, and consumer security scandals in recent history. He has presented as a subject expert on the topic of cybersecurity/corporate espionage and cell phone detection and location at numerous conferences and trade shows around the globe, including GovSec, Counter Terror Expo, ISS Americas, ERII Counterespionage Conference, IEEE, NJTC, Connected World, GSM Mobile World Congress, and more. Schober was a VIP attendee at two Concordia Summits, both held in New York, and was selected to appear in an interview discussing national security.

Hacked Again chronicles his experiences as a hacking victim and the story behind the development of security tools used worldwide.